THE CREDIBILITY OF THE BOOK

OF

THE ACTS OF THE APOSTLES

The Credibility

OF THE BOOK OF

The Acts of the Apostles

BEING

THE HULSEAN LECTURES FOR 1900–1901

BY

FREDERIC HENRY CHASE, D.D.

PRESIDENT OF QUEENS' COLLEGE,
AND NORRISIAN PROFESSOR OF DIVINITY, CAMBRIDGE

Eugene, Oregon

Wipf and Stock Publishers
199 W 8th Ave, Suite 3
Eugene, OR 97401

The Credibility of the Book of the Acts of the Apostles
Being the Hulsean Lectures for 1900-1901
By Chase, Frederic Henry
ISBN: 1-59752-264-3
Publication date 6/14/2005
Previously published by Macmillan and Co., 1902

TO

THE FELLOWS

OF

QUEENS' COLLEGE, CAMBRIDGE

WITH GRATITUDE AND AFFECTION

PREFACE

THE subject for the Hulsean Lectures 1900-1901 was chosen under the conviction that the credibility of the Book of the Acts of the Apostles is second only in importance to the credibility of the Gospels, and that the final verdict must be based on a rigorous and repeated examination of the main course of the narrative and of the types of Apostolic teaching which the Book professes to embody.

It is impossible in four lectures to deal with so large a subject with anything like completeness or thoroughness. Even within the narrow limits which I have marked out for myself, much has been left unsaid. The character of these lectures, for example, prevented me from examining with any minuteness the language of the Book. For some time I have been working at the Acts in preparation for the volume on that Book in *The International Critical Commentary*; and I hope that, if I am allowed to complete that volume, I may in it have an opportunity for the fuller and more detailed discussion of many points on which I have been able in the following pages only to touch. Meantime, I may be permitted to say that the study which I have been able to give to the Book confirms my belief that in it we have a truthful and trustworthy history.

I am deeply conscious of the responsibility which rests on any one who attempts to interpret the records of the Apostolic age. These records from many points of view are of priceless value to the Church of to-day. But minute and patient investigation is the only foundation on which we can securely build the edifice of spiritual instruction. Honesty, accuracy, and reverence are the essential qualifications of the Biblical critic. One who owes a debt which he can never adequately acknowledge to the three great teachers whom during the last half century God has given to Cambridge, the last of whom has but lately ended his earthly work, has had in these respects the highest ideal set

PREFACE ix

before him; and he knows how far he falls short of it.

The last of the four lectures was delivered in St. Mary's Church at a time of profound national sorrow. I have ventured to retain, as a memorial of an historic Sunday, the words, inadequate as they must appear, in which I referred to her late Majesty, Queen Victoria. At the close of the third lecture it was my duty to speak of the late Bishop of London, the sense of the greatness of whose loss to the Church time does not diminish; these few paragraphs also I have printed.

The pleasant task remains of expressing my sincere gratitude to the Rev. A. Wright, M.A., Vice-President of Queens' College, for much valuable help; to the Rev. R. H. Kennett, M.A., Fellow of Queens' College, for answering my questions as to certain Aramaic words; to Mr. A. B. Cook, M.A., late Fellow of Trinity College, for some suggestions which he allows me to embody in the notes on the fourth lecture; to the Rev. G. A. S. Schneider, M.A., of Gonville and Caius College; and to Rev. C. A. Phillips, M.A., of King's College, who with characteristic kindness have on this, as on former occasions, helped me by their criticism in the correction of the proofs. I need hardly add that none of these friends is in any way responsible for the opinions expressed in these lectures, still less for any errors or inaccuracies which may be found in them.

CAMBRIDGE,
Easter Eve, 1902

CONTENTS

LECTURE I

INTRODUCTION. THE DAY OF PENTECOST . . 3

Statement of subject 3. Intrinsic importance of the Book of the Acts 3 f. Prominence of questions relating to it of late years 4-8; (*a*) "Western" text 5 ff., (*b*) archæology 7 f., (*c*) *Quellenkritik* 8, (*d*) Christian doctrine and institutions 8.

Two views of the Book 8-14—(*a*) largely legendary 9, (*b*) the work of St. Luke, a substantially accurate history 9 ff. ; four lines of evidence—(i.) reception in the Church 10 f., (ii.) St. Paul's Epistles 11, (iii.) "we-sertions" 11 ff., (iv.) traces of medical phraseology 13 f.

"Sources" of the Book 14-24 ; (*a*) theories of literary sources not proven 15 f., (*b*) evidence of Preface to St. Luke's Gospel 16 ff., (*c*) St. Luke and the actors in the history, St. Paul 19 f., Philip 20, Elders at Jerusalem 21, St. Mark 21 f., St. Peter 22 ff.

Standard of judgment 24 ff. ; relation of the Book to St. Paul's Epistles 26 f. ; summary 27 f.

The "traditional" theory to be tested by examination of the Book 28 f. ; plan and purpose of the Book 29 f.

I. The Day of Pentecost 30-44. 1. The Temple the scene

xii HULSEAN LECTURES

of the Pentecostal history 30 ff. 2. "Tongues like as of fire" 33 ff. 3. The gift of tongues 35 ff. 4. Significance of the Day of Pentecost 40 ff.

LECTURE II

THE EXPANSION OF THE CHURCH 47

The Lord's command 47 ff. Stages of advance (Jerusalem to Rome), 49 ff. Inclusion of Gentiles in the Church 53. Does the history appear to be a fiction? 53.

Jewish ideas as to "the nations" in Old Testament 54 f., in later literature 55 f., the position of our Lord 56 ff.; thus the writer had no current expectation to guide invention—fact or pure fiction 58 f. In earliest speeches scarcely a reference to the Gentiles 59 f.

The history of the expansion 61-101. (1) The Church at Jerusalem 61-65. No Apostolic policy of advance 61, events connected with St. Stephen 61 f.; effects inwardly and outwardly 63 ff. (2) The Church of Palestine 65-74. The work of Philip 65 ff., conversion of Saul of Tarsus—different accounts 68 ff. (3) The Church of the world 75-101. (*a*) The breaking up of the Apostolic College 75 f., St. Peter's mission to Cornelius 76 ff., his vision 78 f., the Pentecost of the Gentile world 79 f., its meaning not recognised at Jerusalem 80, St. Peter's characteristic work now ended 80 f. (*b*) The Syrian Antioch 81, the Church there at first Jewish 81 ff., Saul of Tarsus 84, the nickname *Christian* 84 ff. (*c*) The mission of Barnabas and Saul 86, their work at Cyprus 86 f., the decision to evangelize the Gentiles 87 ff. (*d*) The position of the Gentiles in the Church 90-101, the controversy 90 f., (1) relation of the account in the Acts to that in the Epistle to the Galatians 91 ff., (2) genuineness of Acts xv. 23 ff., 93 ff., (α) form 94 f., (β) silences 95, (γ) restrictive clauses 95 ff., (*e*) St. Paul's subsequent work 98 ff.

CONTENTS

LECTURE III

THE WITNESS OF ST. PETER 105

Different views as to the record of the speeches 106 ff., two necessarily modifying influences, (*a*) the process of editing 108 ff., (*b*) the transmission of the report 110 ff., possible use of shorthand reports 111 ff., the preservation of other speeches to which this theory is inapplicable 113 ff., the original language of St. Peter's speeches probably Greek 114 ff., their substance remembered because it was the turning-point of many lives and became the subject of after instruction 117 ff., possible influence of written narratives 119 f., St. Luke's personal communication with St. Paul and St. Peter 120 f.

The speeches of St. Peter 122-159, (1) Their Judaic setting 122 ff., their conception of the Work and Person of our Lord 125 ff., the Messianic hope 125 ff., use of the language of this hope in these speeches 129 ff., especially the titles "the Holy and Righteous One" 132 ff., the "Servant" 135 ff. (2) The events of our Lord's life 141 ff., His miracles 142 ff. ; His sufferings and death 144 ff., these sufferings predestined 146 f., they involved absolute humiliation 147 ff. ; His resurrection 150 ff., (*a*) evidences for it 152 f., (*b*) inference as to the Lord's Person—the name Lord 154 ff. ; conclusion 159.

The death of Dr. Creighton, late Bishop of London, 159 ff.

LECTURE IV

THE WITNESS OF ST. PAUL 167

The Acts and the Epistles present different aspects of St. Paul's work 168 f., witness of St. Paul in the Acts to be investigated in relation to three questions 169 f., the selection of speeches probably due to St. Paul 171 f.

HULSEAN LECTURES

1. St. Paul's witness to Israel 172-195. No Pauline Epistle addressed to Jews 172 ff. (*a*) At Damascus 174 ff., "Jesus is the Son of God," significance of the title 174 ff. (*b*) At Antioch in Pisidia 178 ff. Two matters of form (*a*) "*this people Israel*" 179 f., (*b*) Pauline manner of quotation 180 ff. Comparison with St. Stephen's speech 182 f. Three main points—(1) The Passion and the Resurrection, comparison with Petrine speeches and Pauline Epistles 183 ff. (2) The Lord's Person—the Sonship in relation to the Baptism and the Resurrection 187 ff. (3) Justification by faith 191 ff., Jewish literature (*Apoc. Baruch*, 2 *Esdras*) 192 f., quotation from Habakkuk 194 f.

2. St. Paul's witness to the pagan world 195-234. Choice of two specimen speeches (Lystra, Athens) 195 f.—(i.) The speech at Lystra 196-204. General scope of the speech 196 ff. St. Paul, silent as to the world of nature in the Epistles, speaks here only as a student of Old Testament and a prophet 198 f., comparison of speech with the Epistles as to (*a*) the general view of nature as beneficent 200 f, (*b*) its witness to God 201 ff. Nothing directly Christian in the speech 203 f. (ii.) The speech at Athens 204-234. The occasion 204 ff., the Areopagus (the hill, not the court) 207 ff., (*a*) the heathen world and its idolatry 210 ff., attitude of St. Paul towards idolatry in the Epistles and in the speech 210 ff., the altar ἀγνώστῳ θεῷ 216 f., St. Paul's view of God's attitude to "the nations" in the Epistles and in the speech 217 ff., (*b*) the doctrine of God 222 ff., comparison of St. Paul's teaching in the Epistles and in the speech as to (i.) the unity of the race 222 ff., (ii.) the unity of history 224 f., (iii.) the unity of human life (the divine immanence) 225 ff., (*c*) the divine call to repentance 229 ff., the Christian teaching in the speech slight and elementary 231 ff., incidental reference in 1 Cor. to St. Paul's sense of failure at Athens 233 f.

3. St. Paul's pastoral speech at Miletus 234-288. Character of the speech 234 f. (1) The past 236 ff., appeal to the Elders' remembrance of his sojourn at Ephesus 236 f., his life ("the plots of the Jews") 237 ff., his work in public

CONTENTS

240 f., in private 241 ff. (2) The Apologia 243 ff., evidence of the Epistles and of the speech 243 ff., nature of the charges brought against St. Paul 246 f., (i.) undue authority and greed (the Epistles and the speech) 247 ff., (ii.) unfaithfulness to the truth (the Epistles and the speech) 253 ff., (3) St. Paul's forecast of the future 257 ff.—I. His own fate 257 ff., (*a*) comparison of the Epistles and the speech as to the journey to Jerusalem 257 ff., (*b*) explanation of apparent discrepancies as to (i.) the collection for the church at Jerusalem 260 ff., (ii.) St. Paul's expected martyrdom at Jerusalem 262 f.; II. The dangers before the Ephesian Church 265 ff., (i.) dangers from without (persecution) 265 ff., (ii.) dangers from within (false teachers), comparison of the Epistles and the speech 267 ff., (3) the pastoral charge and commendation 271 ff., comparison of the Epistles and speech as to (*a*) the teacher's need of self-discipline 271 ff., (*b*) the divine source of the ministry 273 ff., (*c*) the character of the ministry (the pastoral metaphor, the use of the term $\dot{\epsilon}\pi\iota\sigma\kappa o\pi os$) 275 ff., (*d*) the redeemed church 282 ff. The final commendation 286 ff.

Review of the Pauline speeches 288-292.

Summary of the four lectures 292 ff.; conclusion (the "traditional" view of the book is seen to be the "critical" view) 296; the critic is prepared to consider the further problems of the Book, (*a*) historical *e.g.* the reference to Theudas (v. 36 f.) 296 ff., (*b*) psychological and religious (the supernatural element in the Book) 299 ff.

The death of her late Majesty, Queen Victoria, 302 ff.

INDEX 309

LECTURE I

Λήμψεσθε δύναμιν ἐπελθόντος τοῦ ἁγίου
πνεύματος ἐφ' ὑμᾶς.

23RD SUNDAY AFTER TRINITY,
November 18, 1900.

I

"Ye shall receive power, when the Holy Ghost is come upon you."—ACTS i. 8.

I INVITE you in these lectures to a study of the Book of the Acts of the Apostles. Avoiding, as far as possible, the technical discussion of points of detail, I wish first to follow the main stream of the narrative, and then to review the presentation of Apostolic teaching which we find in the Book. No discussion of the first age of the Church, when the new forces which Christ brought into the world had fullest and freest play, can for the devout student be fruitless in spiritual lessons; but the main object which I set before myself is to ask, and to do what I can towards answering, the question—How far does the Book of the Acts bear a consistent witness to its own veracity?

A vast interval separates the day when the

Lord's visible presence was withdrawn from the disciples and that July some thirty-five years later, when the Roman Emperor found a convenient scapegoat for his own crime in the "great multitude" of those among his subjects at Rome whom the populace called Christians, and whom they hated for their supposed abominations. The Book of the Acts is the one document which professes to bridge the chasm. Again, what a startling transition it is when from the Apostles, sent forth by their Master with no controversial equipment but their conviction that the crucified Messiah had been raised from the dead, we turn to the earliest of St. Paul's Epistles, written to Gentile Churches, and informed by a theology which, however capable of expansion and enrichment, was already clear and definite and comprehensive? The only clue which we have to guide us in the attempt to trace the course of this doctrinal evolution is supplied by the Book of the Acts. This Book stands alone as an authority which gives a coherent account of this period, a period unique in the religious history of mankind.

And if this is the essential interest and importance of the Book, there are special reasons why of late years attention has been directed to it.

With *Codex Bezae* in the University Library close at hand, we are not likely to forget that the Acts is the field on which the battle of the so-called "Western" text is being fought out. Since Professor Blass, having won his laurels in the field of classical scholarship, entered the lists, this controversy has involved the central problems of the genesis of the Book. Insisting on the undoubted fact that "Western" readings are extraordinarily numerous and striking in the Lucan writings, Professor Blass infers that the two types of text, the "Western" text and the common text, represent two editions of the Gospel and of the Acts, put forth by the author himself. In what he accounts the earlier and unabridged edition of the Book a reading occurs —"when *we* had been gathered together" (xi. 28)—which appears to introduce the writer to us as a member of the Church at Antioch in its earliest days, and which therefore, if genuine, throws most valuable light on the writer's history and therefore on the sources of his information. It must suffice here and now with a peremptoriness almost impertinent to say that this theory, so attractive as admitting us into the secrets of St. Luke's literary methods, and accepted as it has been by high authorities—by Dr. Salmon of Dublin and (with some reservations) by Professor Zahn[1]—fails to take into account some of the essential conditions of the problem. It isolates the textual phenomena of the two Lucan Books, and it neglects the artificial character of at least many of the "Western" readings. Yet those who cannot accept Professor Blass's conclusions may in the end find that he has earned their gratitude for emphasizing the fact that it is in the Gospel according to St. Luke and in the Acts that "Western" readings are most conspicuous. A prophecy as to the issue of a conflict, which perhaps is still in its earlier stages, may be rash. But I confess that I look forward to wide and important conclusions emerging from the tangled perplexities of the controversy. While the two Lucan Books were still circulated

[1] See Salmon, *Appendix to a Historical Introduction*, pp. 597 ff.; *Some Criticism on the Text of the New Testament*, pp. 136 ff.; Zahn, *Einleitung in das N. T.*, ii. pp. 338 ff. Blass published his view first in *Theol. Studien u. Kritiken*, 1894, pp. 86 ff., and later (in a somewhat modified form) in *Acta Apostolorum . . . secundum formam quae videtur Romanam*, 1896, pp. vii. f.; *Philology of the Gospels*, pp. 96 ff.

together as the two parts of a single work—
such, I believe, is the inference which must be
drawn from the facts—their text was explained
and paraphrased and assimilated to passages of
the Old Testament and of the Apostolic writings. And hence it follows that the "Western"
text is a proof that, before the Gospels were
formed into a separate collection, the Lucan
writings were regarded as belonging to the
Apostolic literature; and further, that this literature was already becoming co-ordinated with
the Old Testament.

On another side archæology has dealt with
the Book. The spade of the excavator has
revealed the secrets of cities in Asia Minor
which were the scene of St. Paul's activity.
The social and political life of the time, and of
the districts with which the Book is concerned,
stands out in clearer light than it ever did
before. The results of such investigations as
these (which lie outside our special subject) are
widely known in England through the vigorous
and prolific pen of Professor Ramsay. Caution
is doubtless needed, lest weapons of untempered
and untried steel should be rashly placed in the

armoury of the apologist. But it may be safely said that the certain results of archæological research strongly confirm the accuracy and truthfulness of the author of the Acts.

Again, during the last decade the minute and laborious criticism of a series of German scholars has occupied itself with the literary analysis of the Book. Methods which had been fertile of result elsewhere have been pressed into the service here. The discovery of the sources of the Acts became for a time the favourite ambition of explorers in the region of New Testament criticism.[1]

Lastly, historians of the Apostolic age and students of Christian Doctrine and of Christian Institutions have at the most important stage of their work been brought face to face with the question, how far the Book of the Acts can be regarded as a trustworthy historical authority.

Now that the extreme position of the Tübingen school has been abandoned—according to

[1] A convenient *résumé* of these theories will be found in Zöckler's article *Die Apostelgeschichte als Gegenstand höherer und niederer Kritik* in *Greifswalder Studien*, pp. 109-129, or in Mr. A. C. Headlam's article on the Acts in Hastings' *Dict. of the Bible*, i. p. 34.

which the Acts was a late controversial romance, the only historical value of which was to throw light on the thought of the period which produced it — there are, to speak broadly, two main views about the character of the Book which deserve consideration.

On the one hand, it is maintained by scholars who reject the Lucan authorship of the Acts, that it was written early in the second century or somewhat late in the first[1]; that it incorporates, especially in the history of St. Paul's later missionary journeys, fragments of authentic narrative; but that, particularly in the earlier chapters, it is an idealized recension of untrustworthy traditions—at best "a genuine core," to use a phrase of Jülicher's (*Einleitung*, p. 355), "overgrown with legendary accretions."

On the other hand, this last-named view is confronted with the traditional account of the Book, that it was written by St. Luke, a companion of St. Paul, and that it gives not an absolutely perfect but a substantially accurate history of the period which it covers. This

[1] Harnack (*Die Chronologie*, pp. 246 ff.) gives the probable limits of date as 80-93 A.D.; Jülicher (*Einleitung*, p. 344) as 100-105.

view, which I believe to be the true one, rests on the pillars of four facts.

(i.) No sooner did a strictly theological literature arise in the Church at the end of the second and at the beginning of the third century than the Book was referred to by the title familiar to ourselves and as the work of St. Luke. This is the case with the representatives of the great Churches—with Irenæus (iii. 13. 3, ed. Massuet), who united in himself the traditions of South Gaul, of Rome, and of Asia Minor, and who, as the pupil of Polycarp, was the spiritual grandson of St. John; with the author of the Muratorian fragment, possibly Hippolytus, speaking from Rome; with Clement of Alexandria (*Strom.* v. 12, p. 696 ed. Potter); with Tertullian of Carthage (*adv. Marc.* v. 1, *De Jejun.* 10). The obvious interpretation of this unanimity is that the name of Luke was attached to the Book from the first. If we do not accept this conclusion, there are, I believe, two alternatives between which we must make our choice. We may suppose that by a somewhat elaborate process of exclusion some early reader or some early readers of the Book inferred that Luke *might be* the author; that "might be the author" passed into "was the author"; and that this view was universally accepted. Or we may adopt the opinion which has lately found favour with those who give up the Lucan authorship of the whole Book, that the diary of travel incorporated in the Acts was really the work of Luke, and that the fact of some fragments of his journal having been anonymously imbedded in the history somehow brought it about that the whole Book became universally assigned to him. It is obvious that both these theories are weighted with a heavy burden of difficulties and improbabilities.

(ii.) We learn from St. Paul's Epistles to the Colossians and to Philemon that "Luke, the beloved physician," was with him at Rome during his first captivity, and from the Second Epistle to Timothy (if we accept that Epistle, as I believe that we are justified in doing, as authentic) that the same faithful friend was at his side when "the time of his departure" was "at hand."

(iii.) In three sections of the Acts (xvi. 10-17; xx. 5-xxi. 18; xxvii. 1-xxviii. 16) the writer uses the first person plural. The natural inference is that he himself shared in the experiences which he relates in these sections, and was for a time St. Paul's companion. This "we," thus suddenly breaking in, must not be separated from the "me" and the "I" of the opening verses of the Gospel and of the Acts. In striking contrast to the other Evangelists, the author of the third Gospel and of the Acts at the beginning of each of his two treatises speaks in his own person, and thus prepares his readers for those later parts of his work in which he again speaks about himself. The crucial question still remains, whether in vocabulary and in style these sections so resemble the Gospel and the rest of the Acts as to warrant the conclusion that they are not insertions from some independent document. The matter has once more been investigated with singular care and minuteness by Sir John Hawkins in his *Horae Synopticae*. The result of his inquiry may be best given in his own words (p. 154):—" On the whole, then, there is an immense balance of internal and linguistic evidence in favour of the view that the original writer of these sections was the same person as the main author of the Acts and of the third Gospel." Critics who deny this unity of authorship have abstained, so far as I know, from a close investigation as to the literary and linguistic relation of these sections to the rest of the Book and to the Lucan Gospel.

(iv.) St. Paul, as we saw, speaks of St. Luke as "the beloved physician." Dr. Hobart of Dublin, in his work on *The Medical Language of St. Luke*, has endeavoured "to show, from an examination of the language employed in the third Gospel and the Acts of the Apostles, that both are the works of a person well acquainted with the language of the Greek Medical Schools" (p. xxix.). Doubtless the list of coincidences between the vocabulary of the Lucan writings and that of medical writers needs careful sifting. Words, for example, are put down as medical terms which the author of the Acts may just as well have owed to his undoubted familiarity with the LXX. But, when all deductions have been made, there remains a body of evidence that the author of the Acts naturally and inevitably slipped into the use of medical phraseology, which seems to me irresistible. It is needless to insist on the significance of such a coincidence between a casual expression of St. Paul's as to the alleged author of the Acts and of the third Gospel and a characteristic of these Books which lies so far beneath the surface that only by a laborious investigation has it been fully brought to light within the last century. Dr. Hobart's work has been published nearly twenty years. So far as I have observed, it has remained unnoticed by the assailants of the traditional view of the third Gospel and the Acts.

Such are the two estimates of the Book, which, speaking generally, offer themselves to-day for our acceptance. If we allow ourselves for the sake of convenience to use terms, both of which are open to serious misunderstanding, we may call them respectively the "critical" view and the "traditional" view.

It is natural to turn from this main question to one closely related to it, viz. the problem of the "sources" of the Book. What authorities did the writer follow?

I have said that the literary analysis of the Acts as a clue to the written documents out of which it was thought to be built up is a study which has had a fascination for certain Continental scholars. The remarkable characteristic of these efforts is that they have been independent and isolated. They are of interest as the record of the impressions of ingenious individuals; but they have proved too subjective and too arbitrary to command anything approaching a general acceptance. They have not been confirmed by progress towards a coherent theory. May I without presumption state how my own opinion on this question of the sources of the Acts has been modified? I began the study of the Acts some years ago in the full expectation that I should discover signs of the use of various written documents. The investigation appeared at first to promise success. I found differences of phraseology in the several sections of the Book. But when after a time I reviewed the evidence and asked myself whether it was such as would bear the weight of a theory of different literary sources, I was constrained to confess that the variations of style which I could trace were only such as might be expected in a sympathetic author, whose manner instinctively answered to his immediate subject, or such as any writer may observe in his own case if he lays aside his work and resumes it after an interval.

If then our own resources fail us, let us interrogate the writer himself. It seems clear that before the four Gospels were brought together and made into a separate collection, the two Lucan Books, the Gospel and the Acts, must have been circulated together as the two parts of one work. When therefore the Acts immediately followed the Gospel, the Preface prefixed to the earlier treatise would naturally be regarded as an Introduction common to them both. If this view seems strange to us, it is only because the familiar order of our New Testament prevents us from realizing how truly one the two Books are. That the author himself had both parts of his history in mind when he wrote the Preface is, I believe, the inference which we naturally draw from a study of his language. The words "concerning those matters which have been fulfilled among us" seem strangely poor and indefinite, if they refer only to the life and work of Jesus Christ. An inclusive phrase, on the other hand, was necessary if the subject-matter both of the Gospel and of the Acts was within the writer's purview. Again, the two sides of the characteristics claimed for the primary witnesses become in this view full of significance. Their qualification as "eye-witnesses" is important mainly in relation to the events of the Lord's life and, we may add, of the Day of Pentecost; their qualification as "ministers of the word" is concerned rather with the story of Apostolic work.[1] Once more, whatever difficulty may be felt in interpreting the words "to write unto thee *in order*"—a phrase implying some kind of chronological arrangement (comp. Acts xi. 4)— when it is understood to apply only to St. Luke's Gospel, vanishes at once if the reference is to the whole course of the long history which began with the birth of the Baptist and ended with the sojourn of St. Paul in Rome.

If then St. Luke's Preface refers to the Acts

[1] The form of the phrase (οἱ ἀπ' ἀρχῆς αὐτόπται καὶ ὑπηρέται γενόμενοι τοῦ λόγου) appears to shew that only one set of persons is meant. Compare Acts xxvi. 16, προχειρίσασθαί σε ὑπηρέτην καὶ μάρτυρα ὧν τε εἶδές με ὧν τε ὀφθήσομαί σοι.

as much as to the Gospel, we learn that he knew of written narratives dealing with the history of the Apostolic Church; that the ultimate authority for such narratives was the evidence of those who had been eye-witnesses and themselves active workers; that St. Luke to these documents already in circulation added yet another, because he had had special opportunities for investigating the whole course of the history. We could wish that in this Preface he had told us explicitly the sources of his information. He has chosen rather to leave his readers to infer what they were from his indirect statements. On the one hand, since there were written narratives current, based, as he tells us, on the best kind of information, it is probable that he was acquainted with them and influenced by them. But it is at least true that he lightly passes over his relations to his predecessors in the field. On the other hand, his words "even as they delivered them *unto us*" and "it seemed good to me also, having traced the course of all things accurately from the first," seem clearly to imply that his own special qualification for his task (over and above any immediate knowledge of events which he may have had) lay in his personal intercourse with the actors in the scenes which he relates. Can we then with certainty, or with real probability, point to St. Luke's having been brought into contact with those whose testimony, taken together, would cover the whole field of the Acts?

St. Paul himself is without doubt the most obvious and the most important witness. During the three months' sojourn on the island and during the Apostle's captivity for two years at Rome, there was ample opportunity for St. Luke to learn the story of St. Paul's life. From him too, the pupil of Gamaliel and possibly a member of the Sanhedrin, he may well have gained his knowledge of what passed in the council when the Apostles "were put forth a little while" (v. 34 ff.). And here it is well worth noting that, even if the Epistle to the Galatians were the only Epistle of St. Paul preserved to us, we should be assured that the Apostle saw the importance of the history of the Church's past for her guidance in the future, and discerned something of the significance of his own conversion and of his own characteristic work in the fulfilment of the divine purpose. We are growing accustomed to regarding St. Paul as an "ecclesiastical statesman." It may well be the case that St. Paul, with his large views and wide culture, saw how great a purpose the authentic story of "the beginning of the Gospel" would serve in the years, few or many, which lay before the Church on earth; and that, perceiving the literary power of "the beloved physician," he himself laid on St. Luke the task of writing the first history of the Apostolic age. I venture to suggest that it is to St. Paul we owe the conception of the Book of the Acts.

There were only two persons from whom the account of what took place on the road to Gaza could ultimately have been derived, Philip and the Eunuch. With the former the writer of the Acts stayed "many days" on the journey to Jerusalem (xxi. 10). From Philip he could learn the facts about the appointment of the Seven and the evangelization of Samaria, and doubtless also details of still earlier days. Again, the writer of the Acts was a companion of St. Paul when the latter paid his last eventful visit to Jerusalem. It is clear from the narrative of the Acts that he became known to James, the official head of the Church at Jerusalem, and to "the elders" (xxi. 18). The portion of the Acts which follows this notice deals with the purely personal history of St. Paul, and the writer has no opportunity of alluding to his own movements. Since, however, the narrative certifies us that he was with St. Paul just before the latter's arrest at Jerusalem, and since he reappears at the Apostle's side on the eve of the voyage to Rome (xxvii. 1), it is reasonable to infer that he spent part, if not the whole, of the interval in Jerusalem and in Cæsarea. It is needless to insist at length what treasures of information of many kinds were within his reach during these many months. Once more, from the Epistle to the Colossians (iv. 10, 14) we learn that, when St. Luke was at Rome, "Mark, the cousin of Barnabas," was one of those old comrades who gathered round the Apostle. The house of Mary, the mother of Mark, was, it would appear, the home of St. Peter when he revisited Jerusalem (xii. 12 ff.). When early tradition designates St. Mark as "the interpreter of Peter," we may infer with great probability that Mark accompanied that Apostle when he left Jerusalem and began his labours in towns where he had to deal with a Greek-speaking population.[1] Thus the testimony of St. Mark would extend to the events connected with his kinsman Barnabas, to St Paul's first journey, and, we may add with something like certainty, to the earliest days of the Church's life and to all that happened during St. Peter's sojourn at Lydda and Joppa and Cæsarea.

There is then no part of the history contained in the Acts with a primary authority for which, if we accept the natural interpretation of the passages where the first person plural is used, we have not good grounds for saying that the writer had opportunities for personal communication.

And here I venture on what may seem, at first sight, less secure ground.[2] That St. Peter paid a visit of some duration to Rome is an

[1] I may refer to my article on *Mark (John)* in Hastings' *Dictionary of the Bible*, iii. pp. 245 ff.

[2] See my article on *Peter (Simon)* in Hastings' *Dictionary of the Bible*, iii. pp. 769 ff., 778; comp. pp. 790 ff.

opinion supported by the unanimous voice of all early evidence. Only less clear and constant is the testimony that he suffered in the Neronian persecution of A.D. 64. We are thus brought very near the time when we are certain (if we accept as genuine the Epistle to the Colossians and the Second Epistle to Timothy) that St. Luke was in the capital (Col. iv. 14, 2 Tim. iv. 11). For myself, I am inclined to go a step further. Irenæus, a witness who certainly was in contact with trustworthy traditions of the Apostolic age, speaks expressly of St. Peter and St. Paul as *working together* in Rome (iii. 1. 1, ed. Massuet). Such also is the tenor of no small amount of early evidence. Now it is hardly possible to conceive that, when once St. Paul had taken the Apostolic oversight of the Church of Rome, St. Peter, apart from St. Paul, could have planned a visit there. But did he come to Rome, before St. Paul's first captivity was over, at St. Paul's own request? Such an invitation would be a practical corollary to the Epistle to the Ephesians, and in complete harmony with St. Paul's far-seeing policy and large-hearted enthusiasm for unity. If this was so, there is hardly room for doubt that the historian of the Apostolic Church had opportunities of correcting and deepening his knowledge of the events of the first days by what he learned from the lips of the chief actor in those scenes. I do not venture to press this suggestion as one which, with the evidence at present available, can ever attain to more than a measure of probability. But whether it be accepted or not, the likelihood remains that the writer of the early chapters of the Acts met and conversed with St. Peter at Rome.

Such being the writer's opportunities, what kind of history have we a right to expect? By what standard shall we judge the work? To read a good deal of the criticism of the Acts, one would suppose that no reliance can be placed on a writer who does not reach a modern academic ideal, who does not attain to that fulness and accuracy which we expect nowadays from the conscientious writer of an historical or biographical monograph—an exhaustive collection of facts, and a critical use of authorities. But if we try to form a living picture of the possibilities of the writer, we shall look for, and I venture to say that we shall desire, no such laboured precision. The writer has a direct personal knowledge of some part of his subject. As to another period, he retains a vivid remembrance of a conversation with an eye-witness. In regard to a third, he has a record, roughly and hastily written down, of what he learned from one of "the ministers of the word"—the outline or the substance of a speech, the account of some episode of danger and deliverance. As he is weaving all this varied information into a connected whole, he finds that he has lost the clue to the exact meaning of some event, or that he has preserved a record only of the bare fact of a particular journey. His informant is no longer at his side. He cannot communicate with him. At this point, therefore, he has no choice but to set down a meagre and summary statement. And hence there is a want of proportion in his work which is alien to our modern literary ideas. And yet I venture to say that, brief as the Book is, considering the area of events over which it travels, it gives a picture of the characters of the chief actors and of the progress of events infinitely more instinct with life and movement than a scientific presentation of the history could have done. The Book in this respect is like a mediæval Church. Modern mechanical contrivances would have secured an accuracy of measurement and a precision of correspondence which are wanting in the older work. But that older work, whatever its technical defects, has an eloquence and a pathos which are beyond the reach of the better equipped efforts of our own day. We admire it and love it, partly for the strange beauty of its details, partly because of the inspiration which we draw from it as a whole.

One crucial point in the criticism of the Acts lies in the relation of the Book to the Epistles of St. Paul. A writer in the time of Ignatius or of Clement, who was as deeply interested in St. Paul as the author of the Acts, would certainly have known and used some at least of the Epistles of that Apostle. The Acts may indeed be not inaptly called, as Luther (quoted by Zahn, *Einleitung*, ii. p. 408) said, "a comment on St. Paul's Epistles." Yet the "comment" is all the more pointed because it is undesigned. As a matter of fact, the Book contains no reference to the composition of any of St. Paul's letters, and shews no sign of their influence—a strong confirmation of an early date.

We may allow that between the Acts and St. Paul's Epistles there are discrepancies which perhaps do not admit of a formal and complete reconciliation. But they are, I believe, just such as would be due either to gaps in the writer's knowledge which, unless he wrote with St. Paul constantly at his side, would be inevitable, or to that change in the perspective of events which fortunately comes with time. If a son were in some thirty or forty pages to write the eventful story of his father's life, parts of which he had himself watched, of parts of which he had often heard his father speak, we should be surprised and disappointed if, should a packet of his father's old letters be discovered, we gained no clearer view of the sequence and the details of events, no fresh insight into the father's character, no new evidence as to the father's estimate of his relations with his contemporaries at a great crisis long past.

To sum up: it is not too much, I think, to

say that the Lucan authorship of the Acts is the one assumption which gives a natural and adequate explanation (1) of the fact that, at the end of the second century and at the beginning of the third, St. Luke was accounted its author by writers representing the chief Churches of Christendom; (2) of internal characteristics of the Book, the traces of medical phraseology in the language and the abrupt transition from the third person of the historian to the first person of the eye-witness. Further, (3) it enables us to give a reasonable account of the sources whence the writer derived his knowledge of the events, widely separated in time and place, which he records.

But the "traditional" theory must be subjected to a more exacting and a more detailed trial. When Professor Harnack places the composition of the Acts between the years 80 and 93 A.D., it is clear that the difference between his view and the "traditional" view is concerned not so much with the date as with the character of the Book. Does the Book then, when we examine its contents, produce the impression of being history or largely romance? Does it, as we traverse the high-road which the writer marks out for himself, bear witness to its own substantial truthfulness? What then, we ask, is that high-road? What is the purpose and what the plan of the Book?

In the opening paragraph the writer records words spoken by our Lord to the Apostles just before the final separation on the Mount of Olives. He obviously regards them as an utterance of unique solemnity and significance. "Ye shall receive power, when the Holy Ghost is come upon you; and ye shall be my witnesses both in Jerusalem, and in all Judæa and Samaria, and unto the uttermost part of the earth. And when he had said these things, as they were looking, he was taken up; and a cloud received him out of their sight" (i. 3 f.). By these words of Christ the aim and the plan of the Book are determined. It is not an apology nor a series of biographical notices. It is a history, the history of an epoch of revelation. It records the commentary written by events on the Lord's promise and the Lord's commission—the gift of the Spirit, and the witness of the Apostles as the field of the Church's activity broadened, until the Church became a world-wide power.

The fulfilment of the Lord's promise of the Spirit has the foremost place in the record; and the history of the day of Pentecost brings us at once face to face with important matters bearing on the credibility of the Book.

1. The writer of the Book of the Acts, unlike a modern historian, is not at pains to fill in all the details of his picture. He concerns himself primarily with men. Notices of time and place are often perplexingly indistinct.

St. Luke tells us that, both before and after the day of Pentecost, the Apostles were "continually in the Temple" (Luke xxiv. 53, Acts ii. 46). They went thither at the appointed hours of prayer (iii. 1). Their Master's presence there had consecrated it anew for them. Thither they probably had gone with Him on the eve of the Passover, and there they had listened to His prayer of consecration (John xvii.; comp. xviii. 1). As at the Passover (Jos. *Antiq.* XVIII. ii. 2), so at Pentecost, we are told, "it was the custom of the priests to open the gates of the Temple at midnight." There the crowds of worshippers came, that before the morning sacrifice their offerings might be examined by the priests; and there, in the Temple courts, they waited for the solemnities of the Feast (Edersheim, *The Temple*, pp. 228 ff.). Were the Apostles likely to be anywhere but in the Temple that night when the holy feast was already beginning? Does not the writer assume that his readers will understand, without any explicit statement on his part, that the Apostles, like other pious Jews, would naturally resort to the Temple "when the day of Pentecost was being fulfilled"?

When we read the record once more with these thoughts in our minds, the language of the historian is seen to harmonize with the view that the Temple was the scene of the Pentecostal gift. "They were all together in one place." We remember that St. Paul twice uses almost the same phrase of assembling for worship (1 Cor. xi. 20, xiv. 23; comp. Clem. xxxiv. 7, Ign. *Philad.* vi. 2). Again, the word "house"—"it filled all the house where they were sitting"—is the regular term both in the LXX. and in Josephus for the chambers of the Temple.[1] Further, St. Luke tells us that "the multitude came together" (συνῆλθε τὸ πλῆθος, ii. 6). The expression "the multitude" (τὸ πλῆθος) —note the definite article—is employed, both in St. Luke's Gospel and in the Acts, of the crowd of worshippers in the Temple courts (Luke i. 10, Acts xxi. 36; comp. *v. l.* in xxi. 22, συνελθεῖν τὸ πλῆθος).

I do not stop to dwell on the profound significance of the Temple as the place where the supreme gift was given and the dispensation of the Spirit was inaugurated. My point is a much more prosaic one. Note first that, if the Temple is the locality intended, obscurities in the narrative are at once removed. The presence of large numbers of Jews of the Dispersion, and the immediate gathering of "the multitude" to the place where the Apostles were, are explained. The worshippers waiting in the Temple courts flocked to "the house"—the chamber in the Temple—"where

---

[1] See, *e.g.*, Jer. xlii. (xxxv.) 4, xliii. (xxxvi.) 10, 12. 20 f.; Jos. *Antiq.* VII. xiv. 10.

the Apostles were sitting." Again, if "the house" was a house in one of the narrow streets of the city, how could so vast a multitude have come together and have listened to St. Peter's words? And note, in the second place, that, when a writer faintly hints at an important detail which he does not explicitly state,—when he leaves his readers to gather it from the general tenor of his narrative and from his casual expressions,—we may, if we will, criticize his lack of fulness and of clearness, but at least we feel that here we have a sign that he is telling us a real history.

2. I turn next to a deeper and more anxious question. "There appeared unto them tongues parting asunder, like as of fire; and it sat upon each one of them" (ii. 3). Negative critics put aside the whole story of Pentecost as plainly mythical, modelled on Jewish legends of the giving of the Law. Orthodox writers, so far as I have observed, pass over the words without discussion. And yet am I wrong in thinking that some who do not dream of questioning a miraculous element, as we speak, in the history of the

Lord's ministry and of Apostolic times, read these few words not without a distressing sense of perplexity and misgiving? We ask the question, What really happened? What was really seen by the eyes of the Apostles? It may be—I dare not question the possibility—that at this supreme crisis of revelation God willed to "create a new thing in the earth"—fiery shapes in the semblance of tongues diffusing themselves on the heads of men. But, to speak with reverent frankness, such a manifestation seems to be a wonder of a different order from the miracles of the New Testament. It would stand alone. Far be it from me in any way to dogmatize. But are we indeed obliged to choose between an absolutely literal interpretation of these words and, on the other hand, a rejection of the narrative as historical? It is, I venture to urge, a legitimate position that we have here an instance of the mystical interpretation of the divinely-ordered occurrence of a natural phenomenon. May not He who, by what we call natural means, shrouded the cross of the Son of God in darkness[1] have ordained

[1] "The original account (Mt. Mc.) seems to be satisfied by the

that, at the moment when the illuminating Spirit was poured upon the Church, the sunlight of a new day smote upon the Apostles? And if so, was it unnatural that Christians should see a deeper meaning in the sun's rays streaming through the colonnades and the arches of the Temple and resting upon the Apostles, and connecting the sight with the wonders of Apostolic utterance which ensued, should play upon a not uncommon use of the word "tongue," and speak of "tongues like as of fire" resting on the Apostles? Thus the two outward and visible phenomena in the physical world—the rush of the wind and the apocalypse of the sunlight—marked that morning hour of the day of Pentecost as the supreme crisis of the Church's inspiration and of the Church's enlightenment. In the compressed narrative of the Acts at this point St. Luke has blended the language of history and the language of the allegorical interpretation of history.

3. We pass to another difficulty when we

hypothesis of an extraordinary gloom due to natural causes, and coinciding with the last three hours of the Passion" (Dr. Swete on Mc. xv. 33).

approach the problems suggested by the account of the gift of tongues. "In ii. 5-11," writes Professor Ramsay,[1] who yet is an enthusiastic champion of St. Luke's claims to be regarded as an historian of the first rank, "another popular tale seems to obtrude itself. In these verses the power of speaking with tongues, which is clearly described by Paul as a species of prophesying (1 Cor. xii. 10 f., xiv. 1 f.), is taken in the sense of speaking in many languages. Here again we observe the distorting influence of popular fancy."

Let us at once compare the two accounts—St. Luke's and St. Paul's—of this "manifestation of the Spirit."

In the First Epistle to the Corinthians St. Paul asserts that this gift of ecstatic utterance took different forms. There were "divers kinds of tongues" (xii. 28). When therefore he speaks of "the tongues of men" (xiii. 1), and when, to enforce his view that tongues were a sign to unbelievers, he quotes (xiv. 21) some words of Isaiah (xxviii. 11 f.) which held out

---

[1] Professor Ramsay (*St. Paul the Traveller*, p. 370) refers in the immediately preceding context to "the episode of Ananias and Sapphira."

the threat that God would speak to rebellious Israel through the Assyrian invader with his strange dialect, the Apostle appears to imply that speech in foreign languages had *a place* among the phenomena in question. Moreover, according to St. Paul, a bystander was sometimes able to interpret, to translate, what another man said "in a tongue" (xii. 10, xiv. 28). Here it is most natural to suppose that an ecstatic utterance in a foreign language is meant, incomprehensible to the speaker but intelligible to one who knew the language. It is worth noting that, while St. Paul speaks of prophecy and other spiritual endowments as existing in many regions, the only place where, so far as we know, he had to deal with the gift of tongues was one of the busy commercial ports of the Roman world, where men from every nation, Jews and Gentiles, for a time made their home. It is quite in accordance with facts collected by students of mental phenomena to suppose that foreign words heard casually in this meeting-place of nations might be unconsciously reproduced in the abnormal fervour of religious emotion.[1] The probabilities of the case then and the language used by St. Paul alike give support to the view that speech in a foreign language was one among the many forms of *glossolalia* at Corinth. It should be added that, according to St. Paul, these utterances were addressed to God rather than to men. They were mainly prayers, doxologies, thanksgivings.

When from the Epistle to the Corinthians we turn to the far briefer account of the "tongues" on the day of Pentecost, we are struck at once by an important point of similarity. The utterances of the Apostles at Jerusalem, like those of the disciples at Corinth, are described, not as instruction, not as exhortation, but as praise. "We do hear them speaking ... the mighty works of God" (ii. 11; comp. Apoc. xv. 3 ff.). We most naturally, I believe, picture the Apostles, like Zacharias in much earlier days when he was "filled with the Holy Ghost"

---

[1] See the late Dean Plumptre's article on the "Gift of Tongues" in Smith's *Dict. of the Bible*, iii. p. 1561. I am indebted to the Rev. A. Wright for pointing out to me an interesting article by Mr. R. Heath in the *Contemporary Review*, vol. xlix. pp. 117 ff. (Jan. 1886), on "The Little Prophets of the Cevennes." I am glad to find that, in my treatment of this subject, I am in general agreement with Mr. Wright (*Some New Testament Problems*, pp. 277 ff.).

(Luke i. 67 ff.), as bursting forth into "benedictions" drawn from the rich liturgical store of the Jewish Church—such as we find, for example, in that most ancient service of praise and prayer, the *Eighteen Benedictions*.[1] But the Apostles spoke the praises of God in different languages. That is plainly the writer's meaning. Now there is evidence that the authorities in Palestine sanctioned the use of any language whatever in repeating the *Shema*, the *Eighteen Benedictions*, and the Grace at Meals.[2] At other feasts, then, the Apostles had heard strangers of the Dispersion reciting these doxologies in the various languages most familiar to them. Now they in turn themselves, seeing before them Jewish worshippers from many countries, with memories supernaturally quickened, recall and rehearse in the different languages the accustomed words of praise.

---

[1] The student will find the *Eighteen Benedictions* (the Palestinian and the Babylonian recensions) in the original in Prof. Dalman's *Die Worte Jesu*, pp. 299 ff. An English translation is given in Schürer, *History of the Jewish People*, Eng. Trans., II. ii. pp. 85 ff., also in Bp. Westcott's *Hebrews*, pp. 206 ff.

[2] Schürer, *History of the Jewish People*, Eng. Trans., II. ii. p. 284.

Here, too, St. Luke discerned a symbolical meaning. The new spiritual endowment of the Church inaugurates a reversal of the curse of separation. What we may term the very accidents accompanying the advent of the Spirit are a pledge of the catholicity of the Church—a sign that the Church should be the one home of men of every language and race (comp. Col. iii. 11). The historian recalls the language of the ancient story which told of the confusion of tongues (Gen. xi. 7 ff.); and it is plain that his language in recording the events of Pentecost is moulded by the remembrance.

If then we have rightly interpreted St. Paul's account of "the tongues" at Corinth, and St. Luke's record of the marvels of Pentecost, we find that what was an occasional element in the often-repeated manifestation of "tongues" at the Greek seaport was the one form which the gift took at the crisis of its first appearance at Jerusalem.

4. Lastly, passing from details, let us ask ourselves a wider question—What is the significance in the history of the Church of the gift of the Spirit at Pentecost? The disciples,

"the firstfruits unto God from among men," had been disciplined and trained during the months of the Saviour's ministry. That was the period, it may be said, of the Church's catechumenate. The day of the Passion and the day of the Resurrection were the season of the new birth. On the evening of the first Easter day (Jn. xx. 19 ff.) the Lord, in the upper room at Jerusalem, greeted the representatives of the new Society with the blessing of His peace, and then by His sacramental act—" He breathed on them "—and by His quickening word—" Receive ye the Holy Ghost "—He made them partakers of His own risen life. The Church henceforth lived. Henceforth there was, there is, on earth the one Body of Christ. But the divine work of renewal was not yet complete. On the day of Pentecost to the gift of the new life there was added the gift of the new endowment. If Easter day was the day of the Church's birth, Pentecost was the day of the Church's unction, the Church's sealing. To use the phrase which gathers up many hallowed associations for ourselves, Pentecost was the day of the Church's confirmation. Henceforth the life of the one

Body was controlled, guided, inspired by the one Spirit.

Now turn to the history and see how it harmonizes with what reflexion points to as the meaning of Pentecost. St. Luke in the brief interval of waiting which preceded the day of Pentecost places one event, the choice of St. Matthias. The Church lived, and action is the sign of life. The Church acted, acted in the realization that her action on earth must be the reproduction and manifestation of the Lord's action in glory (i. 24, ὃν ἐξελέξω). But communion with the unseen Lord is not sought in an inner and spiritual presence. There is no trust in an inspired rightfulness of judgment. The disciples look for a revelation of the Lord's will through the earthly and mechanical expedient of casting lots. The Church lived; the Church acted. But the action is the action of spiritual immaturity.

After the day of Pentecost all is changed. Henceforth the life of the Church is the revelation of the Spirit. In the Acts the Spirit is represented as the inspirer of the utterances of Christ's chosen witnesses; as giving definite directions at the great crises of the Church's expansion; as controlling the choice of the ministers of the word; as creating and moulding the character of typical workers; as enabling men to discern beforehand the path of suffering which lay before them and their fellows; as touching the life of the disciples with a more than earthly joy and enthusiasm. Thus the Acts is the detailed commentary on all those sayings of the Apostles which speak of the Christian brotherhood, endowed with "the firstfruits of the Spirit" (Rom. viii. 23)—is not this Pauline phrase a definite reference to Pentecost, the Feast of Firstfruits, as the occasion of the divine gift?—as "living by the Spirit," "walking by the Spirit," enlightened by the Spirit. The two pictures of the Church's life in the first days, that given in the Acts and that given in the Apostolic Epistles, are independent. The Epistles give no such information as to the manner of the Spirit's working as could have suggested the details of the Acts. The two pictures are independent; but as we study them with care, they are seen to be complementary and harmonious.

We are the brethren, the younger brethren, of the Apostles and of the earliest saints. We have been born again into the same family of the Father in which they lived and now live and wait. The veil, withdrawn for a brief season, for us hides the workings of the Spirit. But the Spirit is present with us as He was with them. The supreme gift has not been withdrawn. By the counsel of the same Spirit we choose our way of service. In the strength of the same Spirit we strive to do the work which the Father gives us to do. In the light of the same Spirit we see God.

LECTURE II

"Ἔσεσθέ μου μάρτυρες ἔν τε Ἰερουσαλὴμ καὶ ἐν πάσῃ
τῇ Ἰουδαίᾳ καὶ Σαμαρίᾳ καὶ ἕως ἐσχάτου τῆς γῆς.

24TH SUNDAY AFTER TRINITY,
November 25, 1900.

II

"Ye shall be my witnesses both in Jerusalem, and in all Judæa and Samaria, and unto the uttermost part of the earth."—ACTS i. 8.

THE Book of the Acts is the Gospel of the Holy Spirit. But the Holy Spirit works and speaks through men. The voice of the Spirit is the testimony of the disciple. Last week I asked you to consider St. Luke's treatment of one side of his subject. To-day we approach the other side — the widening circles of the witness which the Apostles bore to the Lord Jesus Christ.

"Ye shall be my witnesses." The expression which St. Luke represents our Lord as using, simple as it is, is full of meaning. It has a history. In the second part of Isaiah the prophet draws a magnificent picture of a great assize (Is. xliii. 9 ff.; comp. xliv. 8 ff.). Jehovah puts Himself on His trial. His claims to sovereignty become the subject of a universal controversy. On the one side all the nations are assembled together; on the other, Israel, now chastened and restored—Jehovah's sons brought "from far and His daughters from the end of the earth." The nations are challenged to produce their witnesses and to sustain the pretensions of their gods. There is silence; the appeal is unanswered. Then Jehovah turns to Israel, who has known Him. "Ye are my witnesses, saith Jehovah, and my servant whom I have chosen . . . Ye are my witnesses, saith Jehovah, and I am God." The great assize is now no longer a prophetic vision. Henceforth it is to be wrought out in the daily struggles and triumphs of the Christian Church. The supreme messenger of Jehovah is renewing the ancient challenge. Israel after the flesh by their rejection of Him has proved unworthy of the prerogative once theirs. They are no longer Jehovah's witness to the nations. They have rather passed over into the ranks of those who must receive the testimony of others. The

Apostles, the representatives and prophets of the new Israel of God, are bidden to take up the abdicated office, and, themselves the first recipients of a final salvation, to be Jehovah's witnesses to all the world. Thus Christ's parting words seem designed to mark alike the continuity of revelation and the passing away of the old order.

With the great landmarks of this expansion, laid down by Christ, the author of the Acts deliberately and designedly makes the main divisions of the Book to correspond.

Jerusalem is the starting-point. The Church is first the Church of Jerusalem. Its first home and centre is the Temple.

The Church of Jerusalem grows into the Church of Palestine — "in all Judæa[1] and Samaria." The Church spreads to those who by race and by religion were half Jew and half Gentile. St. Luke carefully marks the beginning of this transitional period with the words: "They were all scattered abroad

[1] Ἰουδαία is here used in the larger sense which it often bears; compare, e.g., Jos. Antiq. I. vii. 2 (εἰς τὴν τότε μὲν Χαναναίαν λεγομένην νῦν δὲ Ἰουδαίαν μετῴκηκε), Tacitus Hist. ii. 78 (Haec [Caesarea] Judaeae caput est), Luke iv. 44, Acts x. 37.

throughout the regions of Judæa and Samaria" (viii. 1). He closes this section of his history with the emphatic note of success: "So the church throughout all Judæa and Galilee and Samaria had peace, being builded up" (ix. 31).

Lastly, the Church of Palestine becomes the Church of the world—"unto the uttermost part of the earth." Again, the phrase chosen, like the words "Ye shall be my witnesses," is an echo from the great evangelical prophecies of the second Isaiah. Nor is it by chance that this expression meets us only once again in this Book—indeed, only once again in the New Testament. At that supreme crisis of his missionary work, when apparently for the first time he was constrained by the unbelief of the Jews to turn to the Gentiles, St. Paul found his course clearly marked out for him by the prophetic words: "I have set thee for a light of the Gentiles, That thou shouldest be for salvation *unto the uttermost part of the earth*" (xiii. 47, quoted from Is. xlix. 6; comp. Is. xlv. 22). The two passages — the one telling us of the primary command of Christ, the other of the resolve of St. Paul—stand to each other in the closest relation.

"Unto the uttermost part of the earth"— the phrase is to us final and prophetic in its universality. For the Apostles and for St. Luke it would necessarily have a narrower meaning. There can be little doubt that to a Palestinian Jew the capital of the Roman Empire would symbolize the idea of world-wide extension. In the *Psalms of Solomon*, for example, Pompey is described as "he who came from the uttermost part of the earth" (τὸν ἀπ' ἐσχάτου τῆς γῆς, viii. 16).

Jerusalem then is the starting-point, Rome the goal, of the Apostolic witness of the first age. If the Gospel made its way along the great roads, and established itself in the cities and colonies, of the Empire; if at last the seed of the kingdom of God, planted in Rome we know not how, was watered and tended there by the ministry of an Apostle, so that it grew into a strong and vigorous tree, then the end of the first chapter of the Church's history was reached. The Church had attained to a typical catholicity. Hence we may say that the subject of the

Book of the Acts is the progress of the Apostolic witness from the religious metropolis of Israel to the political metropolis of the Empire, from Jerusalem to Rome. Twice in the Book itself do Jerusalem and Rome appear as the limits of St. Paul's activity. He is planning that last momentous journey to the Holy City, on which he clearly felt that much depended. "After I have been there," he said, "I must also see Rome" (xix. 21). And as the divinely-ordered course of events is beginning to unfold itself, the purpose of the Apostle is confirmed by an intimation of his Master's will: "As thou hast testified concerning me at Jerusalem, so must thou bear witness also at Rome" (xxiii. 11). As we shall see presently, in the closing paragraph of the Book the narrative reaches a solemn climax—rejection on the one side, unchecked success and hope on the other. In relation to the subject of the Book, the history, when it has brought St. Paul to Rome, is complete. The first treatise of St. Luke tells us of "all that Jesus did and taught from the beginning till . . . he was taken up" (Acts i. 1; comp. v. 22). The second records Christ's last command to His Apostles, and traces the stages of its fulfilment. The two books cover the whole ground (as St. Luke conceived it) of the history of the origins of Christianity—the acts of Jesus Christ, the acts of the Apostles.

Such is the plan of the Book. But in the long drama of the Church's growth from Jerusalem to Rome, the centre of interest is the inclusion of the Gentiles in the one Body of the Messiah, and the way in which this issue was reached.

How far then does the record of the expansion of the Church contained in the Acts satisfy reasonable tests of truthfulness? Certainly it shews no trace of being the working up into a connected story of fragmentary hints drawn from the Apostolic writings. But does it, we ask, bear the marks of being a romance embodying current expectations? Is it coherent, and, on the side of the workers themselves, is it natural—in harmony, that is, with what we observe of human nature when brought into contact with some revolutionary movement of life and thought?

Let us then first inquire how the idea of the catholicity of the Church would present itself to the minds of men familiar with the hopes of the Jews.

In the Old Testament the ultimate relation of Israel to "the nations" occupies no insignificant place. The essential universality of Israel's mission in the world finds clear expression just when the stamp of exclusiveness and isolation seems to be set on the national life in its earliest stage—"in thee shall all the families of the earth be blessed" (Gen. xii. 3). But the glory of this conception became, at least partially, overclouded as the centuries passed by. In the anticipations of the Prophets there are two antithetical lines of prediction. On the one side they draw a picture of judgment, through the terrors of which the nations may, in relation to the commonwealth of Israel, attain to the position of religious helots (*e.g.* Mic. vii. 16 ff.). On the other side we find a series of magnificent representations of Israel as the evangelist, and as the religious home, of "all the nations": "Of Zion it shall be said, This one and that one was born in her" (Ps. lxxxvii. 5); "Nations shall come to thy light, and kings to the brightness of thy rising" (Is. lx. 3).

But as time went on the vicissitudes of the life of the chosen people hardened their feeling towards the surrounding Gentiles, whose religious and moral degradation shocked them, and whose scorn called forth a more than answering scorn. The habit of mind which rejoiced to regard judgment as the necessary portion of "the nations" was strengthened when the Jews felt the iron grasp of Rome tightening upon them. Signs, indeed, of a deeper and holier conception of God's dealings with the world are not wholly wanting. "He" (*i.e.* the Messiah), we read in the *Psalms of Solomon* (xvii. 38), "shall have mercy upon all the nations that come before him in fear" (comp. Enoch xlviii. 4). A prediction in the *Apocalypse of Baruch* (i. 4), standing almost alone in Jewish literature, startles us with the kindliness and the definiteness of its hope: "I will scatter this people among the Gentiles, that they may do good to the Gentiles." But, the history of the chosen people being what it was, it was inevitable that the sterner should be the dominant view.

These forecasts, both in earlier and in later times, are vague, and, to speak generally, catastrophic. The imagery is that of great conflicts, awful days of divine judgment. Even when the hope is kindlier and more generous, the details of the picture of mercy are not filled in. Those who dared to hope that the goodness of the God of Israel would at last enfold "the nations" in its embrace could not discern how the consummation would be brought about.

From Jewish thought we turn to the example and the words of our Lord Himself. Nothing about our Lord's ministry, were we not so familiar with the facts, would be more surprising than its purely national character. "I was not sent but unto the lost sheep of the house of Israel" (Matt. xv. 24). The Apostles, when they leave Him for their evangelistic journey, are warned against straying into any road leading to the Gentiles (Matt. x. 5). It was in a ministry as brief probably as a man's university course and sternly limited to the most exclusive portion of the most exclusive race that the sure foundations of the Catholic Church were laid. With the Resurrection there came the bringing in of a wider hope. The independent accounts in the first and in the third Gospels (not to mention the Appendix to St. Mark's Gospel) leave us in no doubt that among the final commands which the Lord laid upon His disciples there was the one which commissioned them to proclaim Him among "all the nations." But even now, when all doubt as to the purpose of God is removed, there is (so far as our knowledge goes) a remarkable reserve on our Lord's part. When He sent His Apostles out among the towns and villages of their native land, He gave them minute directions as to their conduct. When He sent them forth into the world, there is nothing recorded which leads us to think that He told them anything of the manner in which the great work should be begun, anything of the first steps in that untrodden path, anything of the conditions of the task which He left with them, save only that its accomplishment should be gradual. The difference between the two occasions is not far to seek. It lay, it need not be said, just in this, that now the Lord promised to His Apostles the enlightenment which the presence of the Holy Spirit would give.

The Paraclete would "guide them into all the truth," and in spite of human waywardness would enable them to interpret, and strengthen them to use for the advancement of that truth, the providential ordering of events.

Among the arguments which confirm our belief in the divine origin of the Christian society, not the least persuasive flows from the contrast between the want of any precise and detailed preparation of the Apostles for a world-wide mission, and, on the other hand, the undoubted fact that two or three decades after the Ascension thousands of Gentiles bore the name of Jesus Christ and sacrificed everything simply for His sake. But my special point here is a much smaller one. Clearly the Gentile world had no expectation of blessing through Israel, still less any conception of the manner in which they would be made to share in the consummation of Israel's hope. Jewish forecasts as to the destiny of "the nations" were mostly adverse; they were at best vague and indefinite pictures of a far-off ingathering. The commands of the Lord were explicit as to the ultimate goal of the Gospel, but silent as to the action which the Apostles should take in the immediate future. The historian then who chose as his subject the expansion of the Church, already accomplished when he wrote, must have either truthfully narrated facts which he had been at pains to ascertain, or surrendered himself to his imagination unguided and unchecked by prophecy or current expectation.

What then, in fact, do we find? In the first place, in the speeches which St. Peter is represented in the earlier chapters of the Acts as addressing to the people and to the rulers the great destiny of the Gospel is barely hinted at. Does he quote the words of Joel which speak of "all flesh" as the destined recipients of the gift of the Spirit (ii. 17), and, weaving together phrases of Joel and of Isaiah, declare: "To you is the promise, and to your children, and to all that are afar off, even as many as the Lord our God shall call unto him" (ii. 39; comp. Is. lvii. 19, Joel ii. 32)? There is nothing to shew that his horizon is wider than the horizon of the Prophets. The days seemed at hand when "all the Lord's people should be prophets"

(Num. xi. 29). The Jews from many lands, who were listening to his words, were the pledge of a larger national harvest. The promise of the Spirit was for them and for their descendants and for all faithful Israelites scattered abroad throughout the world, for whose gathering together into one restored people prayer was continually made. Once, and once only, in these earlier speeches of St. Peter does a sense of the wider field of blessing certainly appear; and it appears in the form of insistence on the prerogative of the Jew. The promise of the blessing through Abraham's seed to all the world prefaces the assurance: "Unto you *first* God, having raised up his Servant, sent him to bless you" (iii. 26; comp. Mark vii. 27). Am I wrong in thinking that this preoccupation of the Apostles, as they are represented in the Acts, in the narrow sphere of national hopes, this strange reticence as to the destiny of the Gospel—our Lord's prophecy as to which the writer has set in the forefront of his book, and which before the Acts was written had become an article of religious faith—are signs of a true and faithful portraiture?

From the Apostle's *words* in the early speeches we turn to the *history* of the expansion of the Church.

And first, what of the initiation of the forward movement? "Our acquisition of India," Sir John Seeley has told us, "was made blindly. Nothing great that has ever been done by Englishmen was done so unintentionally, so accidentally, as the conquest of India" (*The Expansion of England*, p. 179). Something of the same kind must be said of the first stages of the Church's expansion. There is nothing religious, nothing even deliberate, about them. There is no consciously decisive step, no consistent policy. The Apostles' action is not the expression of an overwhelming sense of the necessity of spiritual advance. The issue is brought about simply as the result of a divinely-ordered evolution of events. Again I venture to say that the apparent casualness of the history, its fragmentariness, its retrogressions, are a strong guarantee of the substantial truth of the record.

The turning-point comes in a difficulty connected with the charity organization of the

Church. God uses "the base things of the world," the trivialities of a petty dispute, to carry on to a new stage His age-long purposes for the race. There is no relation of fitness between the occasion and the end. The murmuring of "the Hellenists against the Hebrews" —a phrase which incidentally reveals the fact that these two elements coexisted in the Church at Jerusalem—led to the first definite step in the way of organization; and thus there was clothed with the authority of office one who discerned that the present was a transitional state of things, that there were elements of unexpected and unwelcome change inherent in the faith of his Master, and who dared, especially in the synagogues of the Hellenists, to proclaim his belief. No doubt his enemies were restrained by no sense of rigid truthfulness from giving a sharper edge to his prophetic words. But probably it needed little of malicious distortion to lend to his utterances an altogether revolutionary meaning. At the same time it must not escape our notice that St. Stephen's message was rather negative than positive. He foretold rather a breaking with the past than an advance into fresh fields of work.

St. Luke does not, as a modern historian would have done, analyse the issues of events. But, as the story flows naturally on, we feel that, after the witness and the death of St. Stephen, an inward change and an outward change came over the Church.

With this alteration, or supposed alteration, in the aims and convictions of the disciples of Jesus of Nazareth, the neutrality of the Pharisees was at once sacrificed. Gamaliel had cast over them the ægis of his cautious protection. A pupil of Gamaliel now throws his splendid genius and vigour into the work of persecution. The disciples are exposed to the hatred not only of the aristocratic and unpopular Sadducees, but also of that party which enjoyed the special reverence of the people. Hence the fury of the first persecution of the Church. Hence, too, some eight years later (for the fire once kindled was ever ready to break forth in new directions), Herod, whose policy it was to court the Pharisaic party and so gain a wider popularity, "put forth his hands to afflict" the leaders of the Church, and found that his action "pleased the people." In the earlier chapters of the Acts it is an important sign of the writer's truthfulness that, in absolute contrast to that state of things which had come to prevail everywhere long before the Book was written, the little community is described as living in peaceful and happy relations with the people generally. "They had favour with all the people" (ii. 47). The Sadducees "found nothing how they might punish [the Apostles] because of the people" (iv. 21). "The people magnified them" (v. 13). With the death of St. Stephen this period comes to an end. It could not be but that this new universality of hatred had a profound effect on the convictions of the disciples. They could not but ask themselves fundamental questions which they had been slow of heart as yet to entertain—whether Jerusalem would be the centre of the kingdom of their Master; and whether that kingdom would come through the national life of Israel. In this time of silent perplexity, as well as of overt danger, may we not believe that words spoken by the

Lord were brought back to their memory, and that they were trained, when now all men spoke evil of them, to contemplate as possible the passing away of the old order?

The result of St. Stephen's witness, and of the persecution which arose on his death, was the scattering of the Church. Twice in this immediate context (viii. 1, 4), and once in a later passage (xi. 19) in reference to this period, the writer tells us that the disciples "were dispersed" (διεσπάρησαν). The word, I believe, is deliberately chosen. It carries to a further stage that conception of the Church's life and office which, as we saw, found expression in the Lord's last command. The regenerate Israel takes up the ministry of the unfaithful Israel, and now becomes in the providence of God a Dispersion—a διασπορά—among "the nations." "I will scatter this people among the Gentiles, that they may do good to the Gentiles" (*Apoc. Baruch* i. 4).

This dispersion through the sword of the persecutor begins the second period of the history. The Church becomes the Church of

Palestine. A writer drawing on his own imagination would surely have assigned the chief part in this act of the drama to St. Peter, or at least to an Apostle. As a matter of fact, the evangelist of Samaria is the obscure Philip. With him rests the initiation. His work is confirmed by St. Peter and St. John; and the example of the Deacon is followed by the Apostles—"They preached the Gospel to many villages of the Samaritans" (viii. 25). Thus the great concession is made; pure Israelitish descent is no longer a condition of membership in the Church.

But a further and more significant work lay before Philip. In language derived from the history of Elijah[1] the historian describes how a divine direction bade the Evangelist go still farther from Jerusalem, and take the great road running southwards to Egypt; and there, apparently near the site of the ancient Gaza, the explanation of the command was vouchsafed. A second monition of the Spirit impels him to join himself to a chance traveller along

---

[1] 1 Kings xvii. 2, 9 f., 2 Kings i. 3, 15; comp. 1 Kings xiii. 18, Jonah i. 2, iii. 2.

the road; and one who, both from his race and from his physical defect, was excluded from the congregation of Israel, was baptized into Jesus Christ. The Ethiopian Eunuch was, so far as our knowledge goes, the first Gentile Christian. The incident is pregnant with meaning. But in the Acts the story is told with the utmost simplicity. There is nothing dramatic about it. No word of comment is added to point the moral. Philip, who takes the decisive step, is a subordinate minister of the Church. The writer is at no pains to magnify his office, or to follow his history. Again using language drawn from the history of Elijah and Elisha,[1] St. Luke notes that an impulse of the Spirit moved him to retrace his steps northwards, and that at length he settled at Cæsarea. Thus the Evangelist did not return to Jerusalem, and the baptism of the Gentile convert probably long remained unknown to the disciples there. It

[1] 1 Kings xviii. 12, 2 Kings ii. 12, 16 f.; comp. Ezek. *e.g.* iii. 14, viii. 3. That the phrase πνεῦμα Κυρίου ἥρπασεν τὸν Φίλιππον is not intended to imply a miraculous disappearance is clear from the next sentence: καὶ οὐκ εἶδεν αὐτὸν οὐκέτι ὁ εὐνοῦχος, ἐπορεύετο γὰρ τὴν ὁδὸν αὐτοῦ χαίρων. The γάρ explains the reason why "the Eunuch saw him no more." When Philip abruptly left him, the Eunuch did not follow him.

did not raise the questions which had to be faced at a later time.[1]

One other event of unique importance falls within this intermediate period—the conversion of Saul of Tarsus. In the merciful irony of God, he had been allowed to be the chief instrument in the scattering of the Church. Now he is set apart to make that seemingly wasteful sowing fruitful for a distant harvest.

From a literary point of view the writer of the Acts is singularly bold in giving, within the brief compass of his book, three accounts of the conversion, two of them forming parts of speeches of St. Paul. To tell and to retell a tale for the sake of doing so—that is, that it may be presented from different points of view—is a

[1] I have assumed in this paragraph the correctness of the *prima facie* interpretation of the narrative, viz., that the conversion of the Ethiopian Eunuch preceded the conversion of Cornelius. The relative chronology of the Acts, however, is full of uncertainty. St. Luke here (viii. 12, 26, 40, ix. 1, 32 ff., x. 1 ff.), as elsewhere, is silent as to indications of date. It is quite possible that the story of Philip's work (which St. Luke gives, as he had doubtless learned it from Philip himself, in the form of a continuous narrative) carries us on in time beyond the conversion of St. Paul and St. Peter's visit to Cæsarea. But whatever the date of the baptism of the Eunuch was, there is no reason to think that it became widely known or had any influence on the growth of opinion in the Church.

literary device on which none can venture but a writer conscious of great dramatic power. And no one will maintain that the repetition of this episode in the Acts is the *tour de force* of a consummate artist. Nor, again, does the supposition that the author wished to utilize the versions of the history given in different "documents"—even if on general grounds we accepted this account of his sources of information—explain the repetition. The fitness of the three accounts to the several occasions is a sufficient refutation of the theory which regards them as excerpts from different writings. The simplest explanation is, I believe, confirmed by repeated study of these three chapters of the Acts. In the proper place in the Book St. Luke gives the circumstantial account which he had received, perhaps for the purpose of the history, from St. Paul himself. In the later chapters he reproduces his remembrance, aided doubtless by his own written memoranda, of St. Paul's *apologia pro vita sua* as he listened to it first under the shadow of the Tower of Antonia and afterwards in the Basilica of the Procurator at Cæsarea.

This is not the place for a detailed discussion of the relation between the three accounts of St. Paul's conversion. It must suffice to make two remarks. (1) The variations between different accounts contained in a single book are *pro tanto* the sign of a truthful record. The writer at least has not forced his materials into harmony. The really important divergences in this case are explained by the difference between a circumstantial narrative and a rhetorical appeal. (2) In the speech before Agrippa the Lord's words spoken on the road to Damascus are amplified.[1] The Apostle here seems to include within the scope of his review his own deep apprehension of the meaning of Christ's words brought home to him by his later experience,[2] and, we may well believe, by those other "visions and revelations of the Lord" of which

---

[1] It is worth noting that four visions are mentioned in connexion with the conversion: (1) the vision on the road to Damascus (ix. 4 ff., xxii. 7 ff., xxvi. 14 ff.); (2) the vision of Ananias (ix. 10 ff.), in which we are doubtless meant to understand that he learned his message to Saul (ix. 17, xxii. 14 ff.); (3) the vision of Saul (ix. 12); (4) the vision of Saul after his return to Jerusalem (xxii. 17 ff.).

[2] Compare Bishop Westcott, *Characteristics of the Gospel Miracles*, p. 121.

he did not doubt that he was the recipient (2 Cor. xii. 1, Gal. ii. 1). A single phrase in the Epistle to the Galatians shews that he regarded the summons which came to himself as analogous to the call of the Old Testament prophets (Gal. i. 15, Is. xlix. 1, Jer. i. 5). In the same way expressions used in the *apologia* before Agrippa recall divine words which were spoken to Ezekiel and to Jeremiah at the commencement of their ministry (Acts xxvi. 15, Ezek. ii. 1; Acts xxvi. 17, Jer. i. 7 f.; comp. Acts xviii. 9 f.). We can see how natural, how almost inevitable, to St. Paul was the comparison between himself and Jeremiah (Jer. i. 4-10)—the prophet separated for his ministry before his birth; like St. Paul, sent to his own people on a mission of failure and disappointment; appointed "a prophet unto the nations" as St. Paul was "an apostle of the nations" (Rom. xi. 13; comp. 1 Tim. ii. 7).

With all his wonderful courage of self-revelation, St. Paul never in his Epistles removes the veil which rested on the history of his great change. We cannot therefore check the history of the conversion in the Acts by any detailed autobiographical notice in the Apostle's writings. But his own words in many places postulate some definite and sensible crisis such as is related in the Acts.

(*a*) He believed that he had indeed seen the risen Lord. It is often said that when the Apostle describes the turning-point of his life as the time when "it was the good pleasure of God ... to reveal his Son *in me*" (Gal. i. 15 f.), he speaks of an inner and spiritual unveiling of the Saviour to "the eyes of the heart," of which St. Luke gives a coarse and materialized version. Such criticism is only possible when St. Paul's plain words elsewhere are forgotten or explained away. The metaphor of the untimely birth, which he employs in regard to himself (1 Cor. xv. 8), implies a sudden, violent, abnormal change which brought him weak and immature into a new spiritual world. This strange regeneration he connects with a sight of the risen Christ which, he implies, was strictly parallel to that granted to the first witnesses to the Resurrection.

(β) St. Paul believed, as we learn from the Epistles, that he had received his commission from the Lord Jesus Christ, whom his eyes had indeed seen. In the three accounts of the conversion given in the Acts, however the details vary, however some of the incidents are blended, the words of the primary call are constant: "Saul, Saul, why persecutest thou me? ... I am Jesus whom thou persecutest" (ix. 4 f., xxii. 7 f., xxvi. 14 f.). That summons was an appropriation: "I have called thee by thy name: thou art mine" (Is. xliii. 1).

(γ) St. Paul believed, as we learn from the Epistles, that his characteristic work was that he should be an Apostle to the Gentiles. The responsibility of assuming an office so revolutionary would have been too great, too awful for any man, trained in the traditions of Judaism, to bear. St. Paul did not believe that that responsibility was his. He connects his special work with his primary commission: "God ... called me by his grace ... that I should preach [his Son] among the nations" (Gal. i. 16). And this element in his apostleship is emphasized in each of the three accounts of the conversion in the Acts. At the same time, great confusion has been brought into the history, and serious but wholly imaginary difficulties raised, by a misapprehension of the later compact between St. Paul and the Apostles of the Circumcision—" that we should go unto the Gentiles, and they unto the circumcision" (Gal. ii. 9). It was a natural agreement, laying down a general and practical rule as to the direction of their evangelistic work; but it did not finally circumscribe the limits of their activity. On neither side could the terms of the first commission be abrogated. The Apostles of the Circumcision could not put aside the command "to make disciples of all the nations" (Matt. xxviii. 19). St. Paul would be little likely to forget that he was a messenger of the Messiah to Israel. No one can read the Epistle to the Romans and doubt that St. Paul reckoned himself as entrusted with a gospel to his own people.

With an emphatic and solemn notice of the peace and growth of the Church in Palestine which ensued after the conversion of Saul of Tarsus, the second division of the Acts comes to a close (ix. 31).

The third division of the Book opens with one of those simple commonplace phrases with which St. Luke sometimes hints at an important background of history: "And it came to pass, as Peter went throughout all parts, he came down also to the saints which dwelt at Lydda" (ix. 32). Hitherto the Apostles have always been represented as working and acting together. When the storm of persecution burst upon the Church, "all" the disciples "were scattered abroad . . . except the apostles" (viii. 1). When news came to Jerusalem of the evangelization of Samaria, the Apostles took common action, and, following the rule of Christ (Mark vi. 7; Luke x. 1), they sent to the new converts two of their number—those very two who, we have reason to think,[1] had been companions in the first mission to Israel. Thus the apostolic visit to the earliest outpost of the Church was ruled by precedent; there was as yet no breaking with the past. Now all is changed. St. Peter, unaccompanied by any other of the Apostles, leaves Jerusalem, and makes a pro-

[1] See the article on Peter (Simon) in Hastings' *Dictionary of the Bible*, iii. p. 758.

tracted journey, sojourning at Lydda, at Joppa, and at Cæsarea. Does not St. Luke mean us to understand that now—some six years apparently after the Ascension—the Apostolic College was broken up? The time for tarrying at Jerusalem was now over. If the perils of persecution had lately kept the Twelve in the Holy City, now the return of peace justified their departure. The Christian Dispersion needed their presence and their guidance. Henceforth there is no sign that Jerusalem was ever again their settled home. St. Luke's significant statement at this point about St. Peter prepares us for an equally incidental notice later on. From the Apostle's words at the house of Mary—"Tell these things unto James, and to the brethren" (xii. 17)—we infer (comparing later passages) that, before Herod's attack upon the Church, the presidency of the Church at the Holy City had passed from the Apostolic body as a whole into the hands of the elders, with St. James as their head.

The historian now follows the movements of St. Peter. Though no Apostle was with him, we learn (x. 45, xi. 12) that he had companions, strict Jews, among whom we may conjecture with great probability that John Mark, afterwards known in the Church as "the interpreter of Peter," had a place. At length St. Peter settles for some time "in Joppa, with one Simon a tanner." The place is doubly significant. The trade of a tanner was considered among the Jews as unclean.[1] Is then the choice of this house as a lodging a sign that the Apostle's Jewish prejudices were becoming weaker? On the other hand, Joppa was a half-Gentile city. The authorities at Jerusalem, it is said, laid its produce under a ban as defiled by contact with heathenism, and as unfit for use at the sacred festivals. Simon Maccabæus, when "he took Joppa for a haven, made it an entrance for the isles of the sea" (1 Macc. xiv. 5). The position then of the place looking over the waters of the Mediterranean, and its mixed population, could hardly fail to bring home to the mind of the Apostle questionings as to "those who were afar off."

[1] See Schoettgen and Wetstein on Acts ix. 43. As to Joppa see Mr. G. M. Mackie's article on Joppa in Hastings' *Dictionary of the Bible*, ii. p. 755; Prof. G. A. Smith, *Historical Geography of the Holy Land*, p. 138.

Thus he was prepared for the thrice-repeated vision with its divinely-given interpretation, and for the monition of the Spirit bidding him go with the messengers of the Roman soldier, "nothing doubting."

The vision itself is worth a moment's notice. It springs from the present and from St. Peter's immediate surroundings. Doubtless in the market at Joppa questions had to be asked, familiar enough to a Jew of the Dispersion, but strange and repulsive to an untravelled Hebrew. There are in the vision echoes of passages in the Old Testament on which St. Peter may well have been led by his circumstances to meditate. Lastly, it has all the weird, strange surprises of a dream. The Apostle on the house-top, gazing over the waters, sees a sail—a recognized meaning of ὀθόνη in later Greek—outlined against the sky. The next moment it is no longer gliding over the waters, but coming down from heaven. Suddenly the sail is transformed into a kind of ark, in which some of all living creatures are gathered, clean and unclean (comp. Gen. vii. 2, 8). The divine voice recalls the permission,

"Notwithstanding thou mayest *kill and eat* flesh within all thy gates" (Deut. xii. 15). The remonstrance of the Apostle is a reminiscence of the bitter complaint of Ezekiel when he too was confronted with the command from heaven to eat loathsome bread—"Ah Lord God! behold, my soul hath not been polluted : for from my youth up till now have I not eaten of that which died of itself, or is torn of beasts; neither came there abominable flesh into my mouth" (Ezek. iv. 14). In these few verses we are listening to a man telling the phantasmagoria of his dream.

The entrance of the leader of the Apostles into the Roman capital of Judæa, with a population, as Josephus tells us (*B.J.* III. ix. 1), predominantly Gentile, was in itself a crisis in the progress of the Gospel; and the sequel, the descent of the Holy Ghost upon Gentiles, made that day the Pentecost of the Gentile world. The direct action of God revealed that the highest gifts of the heavenly kingdom were within the reach of the Gentile; that in every nation he who seeks finds God, or rather is found by Him, who finds only to bless.

But, strange as it seems to us, the full meaning of this revelation of God's "philanthropy," to use St. Paul's (Titus iii. 4) pregnant word—God's love for man as man—was not as yet discerned. The Apostle's action, indeed, was on his explanation approved by the Church at Jerusalem. But the words in which St. Luke records their final verdict—"Then to the Gentiles also hath God granted repentance unto life" (xi. 18)—are rather a half-grudging acquiescence in what could not be gainsaid—it is the repentance of these "sinners of the Gentiles" which is prominent in their thoughts—than an expression of missionary zeal and joy. The scales of religious exclusiveness do not fall from their eyes. The disciples are content to allow the conversion of Cornelius to remain an isolated overflow of the divine favour. A great and good cause, if it subverts inherited associations and uproots inbred habits of thought, moves onward with a slow and hesitating deliberation infinitely sad in the eyes of men who cannot in the beginning see the end of hope.

This history closes the ministry of St. Peter as narrated in the Acts. He appears again in the Book in connexion with his imprisonment, and once more at the conclave in Jerusalem. But "the acts of Peter" cease just before the work of St. Paul begins. Doubtless St. Luke knew more of St. Peter's ministry; and had he meant a biographical interest to dominate his book he would surely have told us more. But his subject is the expansion of the Church; and St. Peter, in the admission, under divine guidance, of typical Gentiles into the Church, reached the limits of his characteristic work in the kingdom of God.

From the Roman capital of Palestine the history takes us to the Syrian Antioch—a great city of commerce and of pleasure, a meeting-place of all classes of Greeks and Romans and Syrians, and one of the chief centres of the Jewish Dispersion. It was soon to become the mother city of Gentile Christendom.

Was the Church at Antioch a Gentile Church from the first? The question is suggested by a well-known difficulty of reading. It is the only question of textual criticism with which I shall trouble you. The historian tells us that those who were scattered abroad went northwards along the coast-line as far as Phœnicia and Antioch, "speaking the word to none save only to Jews" (xi. 19).[1] The last clause is added to distinguish the scope of their work from that of St. Peter's mission to Cæsarea, with which the previous section had dealt. "And there were some of them," St. Luke continues, "men of Cyprus and Cyrene, who, when they were come to Antioch, spake also unto the Grecian Jews *or* Greeks," πρὸς τοὺς Ἑλληνιστάς *or* πρὸς τοὺς Ἕλληνας—Which of these two words (Ἑλληνιστάς, Ἕλληνας) came from St. Luke's pen? It is, I fancy, becoming rather the fashion to think that here, at any rate, plain common sense gains an open and decisive victory over its pedantic foe, the esoteric principle of scrupulous fidelity to the best critical authorities. The more highly supported reading is Ἑλληνιστάς (Grecian Jews); common sense clamours for the reading Ἕλληνας (Greeks,

[1] The passage runs thus: οἱ μὲν οὖν διασπαρέντες ... διῆλθον ... μηδενὶ λαλοῦντες τὸν λόγον εἰ μὴ μόνον Ἰουδαίοις. Ἦσαν δέ τινες ἐξ αὐτῶν ἄνδρες Κύπριοι καὶ Κυρηναῖοι, οἵτινες ἐλθόντες εἰς Ἀντιόχειαν ἐλάλουν καὶ πρὸς τοὺς Ἑλληνιστάς (*v. l.* Ἕλληνας).

Gentiles) as obviously necessary. The fact, however, is apt to be overlooked that the reading Ἕλληνας (Greeks) makes the historian contradict himself. The evangelists in question were, he tells us, some of those whom he has just described as "speaking the word to none save only to Jews." The verdict of the context then is the same as the verdict of the scrupulous textual critic. St. Luke, we conclude, wrote Ἑλληνιστάς. But the καί—"unto the Grecian Jews *also*"—seems still a persistent witness whose protest against the verdict of the author and of the textual critic refuses to be silenced. The solution of the problem, I venture to think, is a simple one. Has not a single word here, as in some other passages of the Acts, either dropped out in that very early copy which was the archetype of all known texts, or (more probably) been omitted by the author himself? It is a habit of St. Luke to repeat a phrase (with or without some slight variation) which he has used already in a similar context. Did he not write, or intend to write, here, just as he wrote in ix. 29,

ἐλάλουν καὶ συνεζήτουν πρὸς τοὺς Ἑλληνιστάς

("they spake and disputed with the Grecian Jews")?[1]

It was then simply the extraordinary success to which these teachers attained at Antioch, the third city of the Roman Empire, as Josephus (*B.J.* III. ii. 4) accounted it, which attracted the attention of the Church at Jerusalem and led the authorities there to send Barnabas. At Antioch the Gospel was first offered to the Jews. The Church there in its earliest period was still a Judaic Church.

Two matters of interest for our purpose are noted here by St. Luke. Saul of Tarsus, whose powers as an evangelist to the Jews had been already proved at Damascus, at Jerusalem, and doubtless in his native city, is brought by Barnabas to Antioch. And in the second place we learn now for the first time that "the disciples" attracted the notice of their heathen neighbours. The keen wit of the Antiochenes fastened on them the nickname *Christians*. It is often urged on somewhat vague grounds that the name can hardly have

[1] Comp. ix. 29, ἐλάλει τε καὶ συνεζήτει πρὸς τοὺς Ἑλληνιστάς; xviii. 25, ἐλάλει καὶ ἐδίδασκεν; Luke xxiv. 15, ἐν τῷ ὁμιλεῖν αὐτοὺς καὶ συνζητεῖν.

become current at so early a date as St. Luke here asserts. But indeed does not the name itself bear witness to its early origin? It would most naturally attach itself to the followers of Jesus while they were still commonly regarded as a peculiarly extravagant class of Jews. It is to be specially noted that St. Luke does not say that the name *Christian* was now invented, but that it was now first borne by the disciples. It is probable that it already had been occasionally, and in different places, used of the Jews. What more natural than that it should have arisen, for example, at Rome, at one of those crises such as that of which Suetonius (*Claud.* 25) tells us, when there were frequent risings of the Jews at the capital *impulsore Chresto*? The Antiochenes had heard their Jewish neighbours speak of their *Christus*; sometimes their enthusiasm about the name had been fanned into a flame. But these new-comers, and those who gathered round them, could think and speak of nothing and of no one else. If other Jews were partisans of *Christus*, these were certainly the most devoted, the most outrageous, of his adherents. So in the busy streets and in the market-place the jest passed from mouth to mouth, until the nickname became the exclusive possession of the rising sect.

But to resume the history of the Church's expansion :—After a not uneventful interval of more than a year (xi. 26), in a solemn assembly for worship, the will of the Spirit was revealed (xiii. 2), probably through one of the prophets, that Barnabas and Saul should be set apart "for the work whereunto I have called them." They are sent forth as the envoys of the Church at Antioch. The special characteristic of "the work" still remained undefined. Events, however, were so ordered that the evangelists did not long remain in doubt. The Proconsul of Cyprus (whither, as the home of Barnabas, they first went) was, like Hadrian (Tert. *Apol.* 5), "curiositatum omnium explorator." He had been lately amusing himself with a Jewish magician who hung about his court. When he heard of some fresh arrivals, adherents of some new phase of the Jewish superstition, his interest was aroused. He sent for them and questioned them. Saul at once takes the lead, and Sergius Paulus becomes the first-fruits of the great harvest which he was destined to reap from the Gentile world. St. Luke does not stop to emphasize the significance of the conversion of the Roman magistrate. After his manner, he hints at it by recording two facts. Henceforth the Apostle is known by his Roman name. Henceforth he takes the first place; the band of missionaries becomes at once "Paul and his company" (xiii. 13).

From Cyprus the missionaries cross to the mainland and travel inland as far as Perga. Here John Mark "departed from them and returned to Jerusalem" (xiii. 13). St. Mark is one of those minor characters in the Apostolic Church whose movements throw considerable light on the history.[1] We ask then—Why did he, just at this point, having followed them from Cyprus, desert his leaders? Chiefly, we seem to be led to suppose, because at Perga the missionaries took counsel together, and (in the light of recent events) shaped anew their evangelistic policy.

[1] See the article on Mark (John) in Hastings' *Dictionary of the Bible*, iii. pp. 245 f.

St. Paul must all along have been conscious that his apostolate extended to the Gentiles. At Antioch, when the Gentiles began to take a scornful interest in the believers, the question of his duty towards them could not have been far from his thoughts. The events in Cyprus shewed that the time had already come when he should go "far hence unto the Gentiles." It was determined therefore that the little band should cross the Taurus and enter the vast district of Asia Minor, as yet, it would seem, virgin soil to the Christian evangelist. Here an opportunity of work among the Gentiles would be sure soon to offer itself. For these new conditions of service St. Mark, who was, as many indications lead us to think, a strict Hebrew Christian, was not prepared. He had continued with Paul and Barnabas till their resolve was finally taken; now he withdrew.

It was at Perga then, if I mistake not, that the momentous decision was arrived at. What had hitherto been St. Paul's ideal and ambition —it could not be otherwise with his wonderful conversion printed in his memory—was now to become his daily task, "to preach unto the

Gentiles the unsearchable riches of the Messiah" (Eph. iii. 8). The old things of a purely Judaic ministry passed away; they were transfigured into a catholic apostolate.

Soon the looked-for opportunity came. At Antioch in Pisidia the eager attention of the Gentiles, who, on two Sabbath days, found their way into the synagogue, and, on the other hand, the envy and blasphemy of the Jews, meant a welcome of the Gospel on the one side, and a rejection of the Gospel on the other. The decisive words were now for the first time spoken — what they must have cost St. Paul the Epistle to the Romans reveals — "Seeing . . . ye judge yourselves unworthy of eternal life, lo, we turn to the Gentiles" (xiii. 46). And, shewing that this decisive step had been foreseen and well pondered over, the Apostle adds proof that his action was but a fulfilment of an ancient prophetic declaration.

The issue of St. Paul's work at Antioch was the type of its issue elsewhere. In the towns which they visited in that southern corner of the province of Galatia, the missionaries were cheered by wonderful success. But their success was not among Jews but among Gentiles. And when at length they returned to the great Syrian Church which had sent them out, the missionaries sum up the report of their work in the words: "God [hath] opened a door of faith unto the Gentiles" (xiv. 27).

The extension of the Church to the Gentiles was now assured. The position of the Gentiles *in* the Church became at once a pressing question. It was naturally in Antioch that it came to the front. There the missionaries remained "no little time." Possibly before they returned, their example of speaking the word to Gentiles had found imitators at Antioch. Whether this was so or not, certainly after their return a Gentile Church rapidly developed. It at once attracted the attention of "certain men" who "came down from Judæa" (xv. 1). To them the matter presented no difficulty at all. They gave their views with no uncertain sound: "Except ye be circumcised after the custom of Moses, ye cannot be saved."

With these words we are brought to the great controversy of the Apostolic age. One party demanded that a Gentile to become a

Christian must become a Jew. St. Paul maintained that every man is in the fullest sense a potential member of the Christian Church. Let us stop to remark that no one in the age of the Apostles ever thought of proposing the solution which would find favour in our days. It was never once remotely suggested that there should be in Antioch, or anywhere else, two Churches—the Church of the Jew and the Church of the Gentile—two societies independent of each other but loosely allied, worshipping the same Lord but never worshipping Him together. And yet the line of cleavage was clear, deep, natural, drawn by the Creator Himself. In Apostolic days the conception of many bodies of the one Lord was unknown. The unity of ⟨Chu⟩rch was an axiom about which both ⟨…⟩ ⟨w⟩ere in absolute agreement.

⟨T⟩wo main points in connexion with this ⟨cont⟩roversy claim our attention.

⟨1⟩. What is the relation between the history ⟨of⟩ this crisis given in the Acts and St. Paul's ⟨re⟩ference to it in the Epistle to the Galatians?

That there are differences in substance and in tone between the two accounts cannot be denied. Are the variations natural and consistent with substantial truthfulness? I submit that they are fully accounted for by three considerations.

(*a*) Take the most obvious first. St. Luke was a Gentile (Col. iv. 11, 14). He was essentially unable to enter fully into the inwardness of the conflict. He would regard as an outsider the intense emotion which a call in any sense to surrender the Law awoke in a religious Jew, and, on the other hand, the passion of St. Paul's conviction that this surrender was rightful and necessary—a passion proportionate in strength to his own deep personal attachment to the religion of his fathers. An outsider finds no difficulty in writing a calm summary of a dispute.

(*β*) The history was written long after the controversy had passed away. To drag out again into the daylight all the mistakes and heartburnings of the time, if indeed St. Luke knew them, would have been a useless outrage; and he was not guilty of it. The practice nowadays is, when the dead past has decently buried its dead, resolutely to disinter the corpse, and to write a disquisition on the dissector's discoveries. The reticence of the Acts is not an argument against its veracity. It is an example to be followed. The tomb of dead controversies ought to be an inviolable resting-place.

(γ) There is a whole world of difference between the Acts, written as, according to our working hypothesis, we assume it to have been written, and the Epistle of St. Paul, the chief actor in the controversy, written some five years after the crisis itself, and when that crisis in Syria was being reproduced in Galatia by the machinations of Jewish emissaries.

2. We turn in the second place to the question—a crucial question in regard to the historical character of the Acts—of the genuineness of the letter of the "Council" of Jerusalem in Acts xv. It is part of our assumption as to the authorship of the Book that the writer became known to St. James and to the authorities at Jerusalem as the companion of St. Paul, and that consequently he could not but have had ready access to the archives (if that be not too ambitious a word) of the Church at Jerusalem. Does the letter, when

we examine it carefully, confirm our assumption? The discussion must be condensed.

(*a*) Notice the form of the letter. It is essentially a commendatory letter. It warmly recognizes "Barnabas and Paul" (note the older order of names), and it accredits two other men as having authority to explain to the Church at Antioch the decision of the Church at Jerusalem. In form then the letter was very probably modelled on those letters which were constantly being sent from the Sanhedrin and the High Priest to the Synagogues of the Dispersion—letters such as Saul of Tarsus took from the High Priest "to the brethren [note the word] at Damascus" (ix. 2, xxii. 5; comp. xxviii. 21). This view of the letter is strengthened by the opening words: "The apostles and elders, brethren to the brethren in Antioch, Syria, and Cilicia." The salutation in the letter with which the Second Book of the Maccabees opens, and which purports to be addressed by the Palestinian to the Egyptian Jews, is in this double emphasis on the word *brethren* precisely parallel: "The brethren, the Jews that are in Jerusalem . . , send greeting to the brethren, the Jews that are throughout Egypt" (comp. κλητὸς . . . κλητοῖς 1 Cor. i. 1 f., Rom. i. 1, 7). The letter then in Acts xv. is clearly a Jewish letter, probably drawn up after the form of a synagogue letter.

(β) Notice the omissions and the silences of the letter. There is no explicit statement as to the matter in dispute. The words "circumcision," "law," "the custom of Moses," do not occur in it. The details are left to the oral communications of the delegates. And further, only two phrases (one quite incidental) betray the Christian authorship of the document. On matters of Christian doctrine the letter (like the Epistle of St. James) is silent. Such self-repression as this is absolutely incredible in a Pauline Christian composing a fictitious letter for a fictitious history.

(γ) Notice the so-called restrictive clauses: "that ye abstain from things sacrificed to idols, and from blood, and from things strangled, and from fornication" (xv. 29). Of the common explanations of these words, even of that suggested by Dr. Hort (*Judaistic Christianity*, pp. 68 ff.), it must suffice bluntly to say that they fail in two respects: they do not justify the phrase "these necessary things"; they do not distinguish between "blood" and "things strangled." The true interpretation, as I venture to think, was substantially given long ago by a Cambridge scholar of the seventeenth century, Dean Spencer, in his *De Legibus Hebraeorum*.[1] It is hinted at and receives, in fact, abundant illustration in the works of an adopted son of Cambridge, never to be mentioned without reverence, Professor Robertson Smith.[2] All four words alike refer to rites and accompaniments of idolatrous worship. The first and the last need no comment. The word "things offered to idols," standing at the head of the clause, rules the meaning of the two terms, "blood" and "things strangled," which follow. They both refer to rites current among heathen Semites—"blood" possibly to the "rite of

[1] Lib. ii., *Dissertatio in locum illum vexatissimum, Actorum xv. 20*. This remarkable book, which "may justly be said to have laid the foundations of the science of Comparative Religion" (Robertson Smith, *The Religion of the Semites*, preface, p. vi.), was published in 1683. Spencer was Master of Corpus, 1667-1693; Dean of Ely, 1677-1693.

[2] *The Religion of the Semites*, pp. 295 ff., 320, 324, 325 n., 361; *Kinship and Marriage in Early Arabia*, p. 310. The passages in the O.T. are Is. lxv. 4, lxvi. 3, 17, Ezek. iv. 14; comp. Zech. ix. 7.

blood-brotherhood,". "still known in the Lebanon and in some parts of Arabia"; "things strangled," to certain sacrifices referred to in Isaiah, possibly connected with mystic initiations. These practices are chosen for special prohibition, partly because they prevailed in Syria (the letter is addressed to churches in Antioch and Syria), partly because they were peculiarly abhorrent to Jewish feeling. Thus the two parts of the decision strictly correspond. The Jewish Christians do not lay on their Gentile brethren "the yoke of the law." The Gentile Christians are bidden diligently to keep themselves from all participation in idolatrous worship. Our brethren in Delhi could tell us—indeed they have often told us—how fatally easy it is for converts, surrounded by an inheritance of debasing worship, to relapse into idolatrous usages, bound up as these often are with social and family life. If then these restrictive clauses dealt with the special temptations of converts in Syria, we have a natural explanation of the fact that St. Paul does not refer to the letter when answering the questions of the Corinthian Church. On the main lesson, a scrupulous avoidance of all things associated with idolatry, he insists with reiterated emphasis. A study of the language of the letter of the Church at Jerusalem would take us too far into the region of verbal comment. It is not too much to say that such an investigation sets its seal to the conclusion that St. Luke gives us here the very words of the letter which the envoys of the Church at Jerusalem took with them to Antioch.

The great controversy was now decided. St. Paul was able, at least without overt opposition, to carry out his commission and preach to the nations "the Gospel of the grace of God." Into the subsequent history of the expansion of the Church in the provinces of the Empire, Macedonia, Achaia, Asia, we must not now enter. Nor must we trace in the Acts and in the Epistles that complementary side of the Apostle's mission, so impressively described by Dr. Hort—his efforts "to avert a breach between the Christians of Palestine, for whom the Law remained binding while the Temple was still standing, and the Gentile Christians of other lands; to promote kindly recognition on the one side, and brotherly help on the other.[1]"

We must at once hasten to the closing section of the Book.

St. Paul at length attained his long and deeply cherished wish, to witness for his Master at Rome. He entered the city as "the prisoner of Jesus Christ," his very "chain" being a pledge that he refused to surrender "the hope of Israel" (xxviii. 20). Once and yet again he summons to his lodging the chief men of the great Jewish settlement at the capital. Through the one long memorable day — "from morning till evening" — he reasons with them "from the Law of Moses and from the Prophets," "protesting to them of the kingdom of God, and persuading them concerning Jesus." His failure with his fellow-countrymen elsewhere has its counterpart in his failure at Rome. He dismisses them with those awful words of Isaiah, with which St. John (xii. 39 f.) concludes his record of the Saviour's ministry, which speak of

[1] *The Christian Ecclesia*, p. 281 (a sermon preached at Bishop Westcott's consecration).

the necessary rejection of a people wilfully blind and wilfully deaf. As the first pages of the Acts record the witness to Israel at Jerusalem, so the last tells of St. Paul's final and fruitless appeal to Israel at "the uttermost parts of the earth."

But the divine purpose is like the cloudy pillar of the Exodus. It must needs enfold the unbelieving in a hopeless gloom. It gives light to the new Israel of God. "Be it known therefore unto you, that the salvation of God is sent unto the Gentiles: they will also hear." "They will hear"—it is the final word of the Apostle of the Gentiles preserved by his friend. It is a word full of assured hope—a prophecy of the triumph of the Gospel of the Lord Jesus among "all the nations."

In the last paragraph of his book St. Luke records the progress of the Gospel at those "uttermost parts of the earth" of which the Saviour spoke on the Mount of Olives. For the two years of his imprisonment at Rome St. Paul bore his witness to the kingdom of God and to the Lord Jesus Christ "with all boldness, none forbidding him"—

μετὰ πάσης παρρησίας ἀκωλύτως. These two significant phrases express the duty and the confidence of the Missionary Church for all time. They are a record and a prophecy. They were true of the Apostle at Rome in the first century. They are true of the Catholic Church on the eve of the twentieth century. "As for our teaching," exclaims Clement of Alexandria (*Strom.* vi. 18, p. 828 ed. Potter), echoing the trustful triumph of St. Luke's last word, "from its first proclamation kings and despots and rulers in divers countries, and governors with all their armies — yea, with men innumerable, forbid it, making war against us, and endeavouring themselves with all their might to cut us off. Howbeit it blossoms the more; it dies not, as though it were a human teaching, nor, as though it were a gift without strength, does it fade away; for no gift of God is without strength: nay, though prophecy saith of it that it shall be persecuted even unto the end, it abideth as that which cannot be forbidden—μένει ἀκώλυτος."

LECTURE III

Ἀσφαλῶς οὖν γινωσκέτω πᾶς οἶκος Ἰσραὴλ ὅτι καὶ κύριον αὐτὸν καὶ χριστὸν ἐποίησεν ὁ θεός, τοῦτον τὸν Ἰησοῦν ὃν ὑμεῖς ἐσταυρώσατε.

2ND SUNDAY AFTER EPIPHANY,
January 20, 1901.

III

"Let all the house of Israel therefore know assuredly, that God hath made him both Lord and Christ, this Jesus whom ye crucified."
—ACTS ii. 36.

TO-DAY we approach the centre and core of the problem, or group of problems, presented by the Book of the Acts. We have traversed the main road of the history of the Apostolic age—the events of the day of Pentecost; the expansion of the Church, its progress from Jerusalem to Rome. So far as our investigation has gone, we have seen—I speak with earnest and serious conviction—that the record bears a manifold testimony to its own substantial truthfulness.

The acts of the Apostles are the setting of the words of the Apostles. The Apostles, as the representatives of His redeemed Church, were commissioned by the ascending Lord to be His witnesses to all the world. Our task is now to review the record of the witness which in the power of the Spirit they rendered, and to trace the development of Apostolic teaching from the day of that awful glad farewell to the time when, in the Epistles of St. Paul, a Christian literature and a Christian theology arose.

This teaching, so far as the time at our disposal allows us to follow it out, is contained in the speeches of St. Peter and of St. Paul. Next Sunday, with the lessons of the conversion of St. Paul fresh in our minds, we shall, please God, review the witness of St. Paul. To-day our subject is the witness of St. Peter.

Before we enter upon the details of this special subject, some general points, relating to the speeches incorporated in the Acts, demand consideration.

We are familiar with two extreme positions which have been taken up. On the one hand we find it assumed—and we know that when we are not making an effort to speak with scientific precision it is hard not to assume— that here, though it may be in an abbreviated form, we have the actual words which the

Apostles spoke, and that these words are a final expression of Christian truth. On the other hand it is maintained that, while at least some of the historical parts of the Book are built up on a basis of real fact, yet the speeches, at any rate, are the creation of the writer's imagination —the clumsy invention of a dramatist who makes all his characters speak alike. "The similarities found in the speeches," says Jülicher (*Einleitung*, p. 347), "and the religious standpoint which they represent, are due simply to the fact that Luke manufactured these utterances and put his own thoughts into the mouth of both Apostles. Paul is not moulded after a Judaistic type, nor is Peter assimilated to Paul, but Paul and Peter alike have a Lucan, *i.e.* a catholic, character given to them."

The view to which a repeated study—I hope an unprejudiced study—of these speeches has led me is remote from both these extremes. The evidence on which the verdict must be based is of two kinds, literary and doctrinal. It is to the latter kind of evidence that I shall chiefly appeal in the sequel—the doctrinal differences between the speeches, their relation to what we know of contemporary thought and to the teaching of the Epistles. Meantime, this broad statement of widely divergent views may serve to bring out clearly the points at issue.

In considering the truthfulness of the record we must be prepared to recognise two influences which cannot but have modified the report of these Apostolic words both in form and in substance—the work of the editor and the process of transmission to the editor.

(*a*) The writer of the Acts, if he did not invent the discourses, yet certainly edited whatever record of them came into his hands. He gave the speeches their present literary form. Of this conclusion, antecedently probable, the study of the language of the Apostolic addresses, when compared with each other and with the rest of the Book, is a sufficient proof. How far this editing penetrated into the fabric of the discourses is a question to which no certain and uniform answer can be given. We have no evidence outside the Book itself to which we can appeal. We can only turn to the analogous case of our Lord's words preserved to us in St. Luke's Gospel. Here in the parallels supplied by the other Synoptists we have an external standard to guide and control our judgment. An examination of typical passages in St. Luke, where the agreement of St. Mark and St. Matthew enables us to form an approximately accurate idea of the "source," seems to shew that St. Luke was wont to deal somewhat freely with his materials. Sometimes he rewrites and expands; see, for example, the parable of the strong man armed (xi. 21 f.). At other times he adds a word or a phrase to bring a latent idea into clearer relief, *e.g.* the treading under foot of the seed by the wayside (viii. 5), or the rending of the new garment (v. 36). Or again, he interprets or replaces the words of the "source" with phrases characteristic of his own style or derived from the LXX., or which belong to the category of medical terms. He changes simple into compound words; he introduces phrases of a more elaborate and ornate type. Thus the editing work of St. Luke, speaking generally, gives to his record of "the Oracles of the Lord" a somewhat greater fulness and elaboration and a more distinctly literary flavour and finish. At the same time he is faithful to the original ideas; he does not build upon the foundation of his "source" a superstructure of teaching of his own. It is a fact of deep significance—a fact which warns us and braces us—that seldom can we assert about a saying of the Saviour, "This is the exact equivalent of the very words which came from His lips." Here we live by faith. Here it is the spirit, not the letter, which trains us in the wisdom He came to teach. Here we have need of patience. And if this is the case with the sayings of the Master Himself, we cannot expect it to be otherwise with the sayings of the disciples. For—to return to our immediate subject—certainly the Evangelist, who changed in form and to some extent in substance the tradition of the words of the Lord Jesus Christ, would not hesitate to mould and shape the report, however it came to him, of the words of the Apostles.

(*b*) But how did the report come to him? Again we must confess that no certain or uniform answer can be given to this question.

At some of the speeches (if our working hypothesis as to the writer of the Book is correct) St. Luke was himself present— probably, that is, at the speeches after St. Paul's apprehension at Jerusalem, and certainly at St. Paul's address to the Elders of Ephesus. And in regard to these speeches (with the exception of that *apologia* of St. Paul which was occasioned by the sudden tumult in the Temple) another possibility must be borne in mind. If we examine the speech of the advocate Tertullus (xxiv. 2 ff.) we are struck by the fact that the complementary phrases of the exordium are evidently preserved with some exactness, but that, when the main subject of the speech (*i.e.* the history of St. Paul's case) is reached, the grammatical construction of the sentence is lost in three curt, stunt, relative clauses. To what does this phenomenon point? Any one who has taken notes of a lecture or a speech knows that at first he is anxious and alert to set down the exact words used; but that after a time, especially if the speaker gets on familiar ground, the effort is relaxed, and he is content with jotting down brief and disjointed notes of what he hears. We know that some kind of shorthand-writing was practised among the ancients[1]; and I venture to suggest that it is probable that in the case of the speeches contained in the closing chapters of the Acts we have, more or less edited and elaborated, a transcript of notes taken of them at the time, it may well be by St. Luke himself. It is far from impossible that in the same way the speech at Miletus was preserved. It was delivered on an occasion deliberately arranged beforehand—"And from Miletus he sent to Ephesus, and called to him the elders of the church" (xx. 17). It belongs to a period long after St. Paul, as we learn from the Epistle to the Romans, was regarded as speaking with a widely recognised authority. It was a farewell utterance of peculiar solemnity and lasting significance. Clearly there would be special reasons for preserving a permanent record of St. Paul's words, for the sake both of his

[1] See the article Nota in Smith's *Dictionary of Greek and Roman Antiquities*. Galen (xix. p. 11, ed. Kühn) mentions the fact that the medical students who attended his lectures took them down (ἀντίγραφα μειρακίοις ὑπαγορευθέντων ἀρχομένοις μανθάνειν). It is by no means impossible that St. Luke acquired the power of shorthand-writing in connexion with his training in medicine.

immediate hearers and of the great Church of Ephesus, so long the Apostle's home, of which the Elders were the representatives.

If the suggestion that some of the speeches preserved in the Acts are based on something analogous to shorthand reports has a peculiarly modern sound and seems to antedate the journalistic methods of our own days, this impression is due, I think, to our somewhat supercilious forgetfulness that, in regard to those accessories and embellishments of life which are not the outcome of strictly scientific knowledge, ancient civilisation was not so very far behind our own.

Most of the speeches in the Acts, however, were called forth by the sudden exigencies of the moment. Their interest and importance would not be perceived till afterwards. To them the theory which I have just advanced will not apply. How then can we explain their preservation? How far do they differ, or do they differ at all, from those political speeches of which Thucydides in a well-known passage (i. 22) says that his informants found it hard to give him anything of an exact report? Directly we ask these questions we are conscious that we are confronted by another. In what language were the speeches of St. Peter originally delivered? There can be no question that those addressed to the Jews of Jerusalem were, like St. Paul's speech on the steps of the Castle, spoken in Aramaic. Consequently here, as in the case of our Lord's discourses, we must make allowance for changes necessarily caused by translation more or less free. But the case is not so clear with the speeches of St. Peter at the house of Cornelius and on the day of Pentecost. On the one hand, in reference to the latter it cannot be disputed that Greek was the only language which would be generally intelligible to Jews gathered from all parts of the Dispersion. They could not have been deeply stirred by a preacher speaking to them in a language of which they only knew a few words. But, on the other hand, can we suppose that St. Peter was able to deliver a connected speech in intelligible Greek? The question, I need not tell you, is in reality a complicated one, and the evidence slighter and less decisive than we could wish. I can but with the utmost brevity suggest what appear to me the important considerations.[1]

In Galilee then, with its Greek towns like Gadara and with a mixed population which trade had brought together, Greek must have been to a large extent the language of business. And further, if in Jerusalem, then surely in the commercial towns of Galilee, there must have been Hellenistic synagogues frequented by Jews who had come from the Dispersion, where the Discourse, which followed the Lessons from the Law and the Prophets, would be in Greek. It is unlikely, then, to say the least, that, when St. Peter was called to follow Christ, he was wholly ignorant of colloquial Greek. Again, passing with his Master from place to place in Galilee the Apostle would be thrown with Greek-speaking people to a greater degree than he would have been had he remained in his home on the Lake, while the visits to Jerusalem at the time of the feasts would almost certainly bring him into contact with Jews of the Dispersion. Nor does it seem by

[1] Compare the article on Peter (Simon) in Hastings' *Dictionary of the Bible*, iii. p. 757, and the article on Peter, First Epistle, *ib.* iii. p. 787.

any means impossible that a Palestinian Jew would be acquainted with the LXX. That version must have been in use in the Hellenistic synagogues of Jerusalem and of Galilee,[1] and some knowledge of it could hardly but spread to their Hebrew neighbours. Further, when we consider the use of the LXX. in the Epistle to the Hebrews,—an epistle addressed in all probability to a strictly Jewish Church in or near Jerusalem,—and the familiarity with the language of the LXX. shewn in the Epistle of St. James, a strict Jew whose home was in Jerusalem, it is not an extravagant supposition that some parts at least of the great Greek version were known to St. Peter when he began his apostolic ministry at Jerusalem. There is then much to be said in favour of the view that the Apostle spoke to the crowds on the day of Pentecost in Greek. In the other scale, however, must be placed the clear and precise evidence that the Apostle at a later time took St. Mark to be his companion in his journeys and his interpreter. Such a notice

[1] Compare Swete, *An Introduction to the Old Testament in Greek*, p. 29.

certainly implies that St. Peter, at least in the earliest days of the Gospel, could not speak fluently and connectedly in Greek. I confess that, when I try to harmonize the different lines of evidence and to realize the scene in the courts of the Temple, I am inclined to hazard the conjecture that the apostolic utterance was less of a set continuous speech than St. Luke's account would at first sight lead us to suppose; that, as in the case of our Lord's discourses, something of dialogue was mingled with the address; that possibly Aramaic and Greek were both used, as the Apostle turned from this group among his hearers to that; and that questions and answers gave opportunity for explanation and interpretation.

But whatever was the language in which St. Peter spoke, and whatever the exact form of this earliest Christian sermon, how can we reasonably suppose that it and the other speeches at Jerusalem were preserved? Common experience tells us how much a man recalls of the matter and of the actual language of a conversation or of a sermon which has deeply and permanently influenced him. They are wrought into the fabric of his mind. This is so even in the hurry of modern European life; much more so with the meditative minds of the East. And further, if many persons have been influenced by the same words of the same speaker, and in consequence have adopted a new fashion of life, their sympathy in their common cause will inevitably lead them to speak together of what was the occasion of their great resolve, and thus a common memory will fashion itself into a common tradition. Nor is this all. The truths proclaimed by St. Peter in his sermons in the Temple became at once the subject of the "apostles' teaching," in which the brethren "continued steadfast" (ii. 42). The witness of the Old Testament to the suffering and exalted Messiah and to the promise of the Holy Spirit would be emphasized again and again in the oral instruction given to the disciples. The great facts of Christ's life, which on the day of their regeneration had laid so powerful a hold on their hearts and consciences, would be affirmed and reaffirmed. And this instruction would be given and received by men who were penetrated by the Messianic hope, and who recognised in their new faith a fresh consecration of the language in which that hope found expression. And here we must notice a fact of far-reaching import. From the day of Pentecost onwards there must have existed in the Church of Jerusalem two classes of converts—Hebrews and Hellenists. The instruction given to the former in Aramaic would among the latter assume a Greek dress, and thus there would grow up a Greek tradition of what St. Peter said in his memorable utterances; and this Greek tradition, we may reasonably conjecture, was the basis of St. Luke's record of his words. Thus, to sum up, through the later instruction based upon them, the original Apostolic utterances become a permanent possession, while at the same time the form in which they were remembered could not but to some extent be moulded and shaped by the very process whereby they were imprinted upon the memory of the disciples.

Two other possible factors in the preservation in their present form of the speeches of St. Peter must not be forgotten.

In the first place, St. Luke refers in the Preface to earlier written narratives. In considering how the Apostolic words were handed down, we must take into account the presence among the earliest disciples of Joseph of Arimathæa, Nicodemus, Barnabas, and of others like them. Even from the point of view of the Sanhedrin such men could not be accounted as "unlearned and ignorant." Some of these may well have preserved in writing some record of St. Peter's witness to the Lord.

In the second place, it is even more important that we should remind ourselves of the evidence which we have as to St. Luke's personal communication with the speakers themselves. It is hard to suppose that the Evangelist wrote down his report of St. Paul's words at Antioch, Lystra, Athens, and Miletus, without reference to the Apostle himself. That St. Paul was his one and only authority for these speeches is an obvious conjecture which, the more we study the speeches in connexion with the Pauline Epistles, the more we are inclined to regard as natural and adequate. But the case is less obvious in reference to

St. Peter. The student of St. Peter's speeches in the Acts, and of his Epistle to the Churches of Asia Minor, cannot fail to notice parallels between the reported and the written words of the Apostle. It is not now possible to discuss these similarities in detail, and I have no wish to lay overmuch stress on them. But there is one coincidence in expression and thought too remarkable to pass over. In the Epistle and in one of the speeches, Christ, who with the Father is the object of man's faith or faithfulness, is described as the channel of its bestowal—ἡ πίστις ἡ δι' αὐτοῦ (Acts iii. 16), τοὺς δι' αὐτοῦ πιστοὺς εἰς θεόν (1 Peter i. 21). We may well hesitate to build an imposing edifice of inference on a slight foundation; but I confess that this parallel between the two documents, taken in connexion with the others to which I have alluded, suggests that St. Luke's authority for, or St. Luke's own version of, the Petrine speeches passed through St. Peter's hands, and that some touches in them are due to him. We have already seen (pp. 22 ff.) that there is a strong probability that St. Luke met St. Peter at Rome.

So far then we have seen that a reasonable account can be given of the preservation of the Apostolic speeches contained in the Acts; but that, on the other hand, we must be prepared to allow that the original utterances have been modified by translation (in some cases), by the process of transmission, by the moulding hand of the writer of the Book.

We pass at once to the Petrine speeches themselves—the speech on the day of Pentecost ("Jesus the Nazarene, the enthroned Messiah"); the speech in Solomon's Portico ("Jesus, the glorified Servant, the Restorer"); the witness on two occasions before the Sanhedrin ("Jesus, rejected by the rulers, raised by God to be the Saviour"); the speech in the house of Cornelius ("Jesus, the Lord of all ").

I. Pausing for a moment on the threshold of the doctrinal teaching of these speeches, notice how consistently Judaic is their setting. Thus take the phrases of appeal—"Israelites, hear these words," and the like. They belong to a type of phrase very familiar to a devout Jew through the opening words of the *Shema*, "Hear, O Israel." Again, note the forms of address—ἄνδρες Ἰσραηλεῖται, ἄνδρες ἀδελφοί, υἱοὶ γένους Ἀβραάμ (to quote one phrase from St. Paul's synagogue address),—all these, I believe, are instances of the homiletic formulas of the synagogue. They have their counterparts in the so-called *Fourth Book of the Maccabees*—"almost the solitary example," as Ewald says (*History*, v. p. 485, Eng. trans.), "of a Jewish sermon." This book, I may note in passing, contains (viii. 19) the one instance outside the Acts, so far as my search has gone, of the familiar phrase ἄνδρες ἀδελφοί—a phrase so simple and apparently uninteresting, but in reality exemplifying that union of Jewish thought and Greek expression which was characteristic of the Dispersion. Further illustration would, I believe, confirm the verdict that in these phrases of appeal and of address we have echoes from the Hellenistic synagogues. Or, to take instances of a somewhat different kind, the phrase "the whole house of Israel," used with marked significance once in the Acts (ii. 36), and found nowhere else in the

New Testament, is not infrequent in Jewish prayers; it occurs three times in the *Kaddish*. Again, the opening words of St. Peter's second speech, "The God of Abraham, and of Isaac, and of Jacob, the God of our fathers" (iii. 13), is the solemn formula with which the first of the *Eighteen Benedictions* begins. Again, the expression "sons of the covenant" (iii. 25), in the same speech, occurs in the *Psalms of Solomon* (xvii. 17; cf. Ezek. xxx. 5), and is analogous to the phrase "a son of the law," which meets us, apparently for the first time, in the *Apocalypse of Baruch* (xlvi. 4).

These and similar expressions have, if I mistake not, an interest and a meaning deeper than those which belong to mere linguistic curiosities. They are relics of a phase of Jewish life of which comparatively few traces now remain. Certainly a writer evolving these speeches out of his own imagination, when the gulf which separated the Synagogue from the Church was wide and was daily growing wider, would not have been likely to introduce them so freely and so naturally. They carry us back, I believe, beyond the editing work of the Gentile

Evangelist to the Hellenistic version or tradition of the speeches, which, as we saw reason to think, St. Luke used as his authority.

The consideration of these links between the Acts and Jewish life brings us to a much more important subject—the conception of the Person and Work of our Lord found in the Petrine speeches of the Acts. In these speeches, if they are substantially genuine, we have the meeting of the streams. The one has long flowed through the soil of human history; the other has but just welled forth from the pure fountain. The one is the Jewish doctrine of the Messiah; the other the redemptive work of Jesus Christ, now complete. Do these speeches answer to their alleged unique position in the history of religious thought?

What was the Messianic hope then current? The question can here be answered only in outline; but for clearness some answer, however brief, is necessary.

The group of national and religious aspirations and beliefs which are included under the term *the Messianic hope*, as far as we are now concerned with them, became active during the last century and a half before the birth of Christ. The foundation of this superstructure was laid in the Old Testament portraiture of the three closely-related actors (if I may use the term in this connexion) in the drama of Israel's history — (1) Jehovah, holy in His essential nature, righteous in His kingly dealings with men, ruling over His people and leading them on to a final and complete triumph; (2) the nation itself, Jehovah's son and servant, ideally holy and righteous as Jehovah Himself; (3) the king, the χριστὸς βασιλεύς, the day of whose anointing was ideally the day in which he, the nation's representative, was born into a new relation of sonship towards Jehovah. Different elements in the hope of ultimate victory and exaltation were brought out now by this prophet, now by that. It was in prosaic days of failure that they were welded together into an idea which moved and quickened the whole nation. For this rise of the Messianic hope, as it appears to us in New Testament times, we may perhaps say, though an artificial analysis is always partial and incomplete, that there were three main causes—literary, political, religious. (1) The Messiah appears as the chief figure in an eschatological literature, to which the sense of national failure gave birth. (2) The Messiah, the divine King after the Davidic type, fills the place in the political hopes of the nation left vacant by the degeneracy of the later Asmonean princes. (3) The Messiah becomes the centre of a deep religious belief in Jehovah's activity on behalf of His people, a belief which was a reaction from, and a protest against, the scholasticism of the Scribes and the materialism of the Sadducees. Thus in the ideas which gathered round the figure of the Messiah there were two essential elements —deliverance and reformation; salvation from servitude, and a cleansing from the sins which defiled, and from the sinful ones who degraded, the religious life of the people.

It would be a mistake, of course, to suppose that there was a uniform advance in the Jewish hope of the Messiah. The idea necessarily developed differently in different classes of minds. Thus Professor Dalman (*Die Worte Jesu*, p. 244) points out that there were two conceptions which can be traced as existing side by side at the time of the Advent—an older view which regarded the Messiah as prince among a people whose deliverer had been God; a more recent belief according to which the Messiah himself was the redeemer, and afterwards the ruler, of the nation. And if we must allow for variations, there is another and a more serious error against which we must be on our guard. We know how the Messianic belief had its consummation in the Christian creed. We know how, when their national hope became almost extinct, the Jews with pathetic persistency clung to their belief that Messiah would come, but were constrained by the logic of events to transfer their conception of Messiah to a less earthly sphere. We must beware then lest into the Messianic expectation which was prevalent in our Lord's days we read a religious and spiritual consciousness which did not as a matter of fact belong to it. "The office of the Messiah," to quote from Professor Dalman once more (p. 245), "did not lie in his being an exemplar, or a moral teacher, or one who makes atonement, still less in his being a dispenser of the Divine Spirit; it consisted simply in this—his reigning over Israel as a king who answers to the divine will."

Let us now examine some points in the earlier speeches of the Acts, among which, for our present purpose, we may include St. Paul's address in the synagogue of Antioch. The speakers, who believed Jesus to be the Christ, and the hearers were alike in this, that they were familiar with the ideas and the language of the Messianic hope. If the speeches are in any real sense authentic, they will be found to be impregnated with these ideas; their statements and appeals will be expressed in this language.

There is a group of phrases in the Apostolic speeches which at first strikes the reader as simply archaic—echoes from the early records of Israel's history: "The God of our fathers raised up Jesus" (v. 30), "a Prince and a Saviour" ($ἀρχηγὸν\ καὶ\ σωτῆρα$, v. 31), "God brought unto Israel a Saviour, Jesus" (xiii. 23). We turn to the Book of Judges and we find that similar phrases are used almost as an historical formula: "The LORD raised up a saviour to the children of Israel, who saved them" (ἤγειρεν Κύριος σωτῆρα τῷ Ἰσραὴλ καὶ ἔσωσεν αὐτούς, iii. 9). The word "captain," "prince" (ἀρχηγός), occurs several times in the Pentateuch and in the Book of Judges (though the Greek texts vary) in reference to the military leaders of Israel. Our first impulse is to set down these expressions as instances of St. Luke's constant habit of using the language of the LXX. But the Book of Judges is, we must confess, remote from the work of the Lord Jesus Christ; it is not that part of the Old Testament to which the mind of a Christian writer would instinctively turn for adumbrations of His redemptive work. There are, however, in fact abundant proofs that such language, derived from the history of Israel's earliest deliverances, was part of the current phraseology—liturgical and literary—of the Messianic hope. In the *Eighteen Benedictions* (xi.), for example, the promise of Isaiah becomes a prayer: "Restore our judges as at the first." In the oldest portion of the *Sibylline Oracles* (iii. 652 ff.) and in the *Psalms of Solomon*—to refer only to two specimens of extra-Canonical Jewish literature—the Messiah is depicted as a royal captain triumphing over the ungodly powers. "Behold, O Lord, and raise up unto them their king, the son of David. . . . and gird him with strength that he may break in pieces them that rule unjustly. . . . He shall destroy the ungodly nations with the word of his mouth" (Pss. Sol. xvii. 23 ff.[1]). In this connexion in particular the words "salvation," "saviour" (deliverance, deliverer), so precious in their known—ay, and in their to us as yet unknown and unimagined, treasuries of hope, are well worthy of study. Jesus the Nazarene is the Saviour; "in none other is there salvation" (iv. 12). The occasion of these last words is the healing of the cripple. To St. Peter and to his hearers the close connexion of healing and salvation—the Messianic salvation (comp. Pss. Sol. x. 9)—would be no strange thought. "Heal us"—I quote from one form of the *Eighteen Benedictions*,—"Heal us, Jehovah, and we shall be healed. Save us and we shall be saved. . . . Yea, cure and heal all our diseases and all our pains and all our wounds. For Thou,

[1] See Ryle and James' note on ver. 26.

O God, art a compassionate and faithful healer. Blessed art Thou, Jehovah, even He that healeth the diseased of His people Israel.[1]" The word *salvation*, as St. Peter uses it, is still coloured by the lower associations of national aspiration—deliverance, restoration, unity; it is the divine gift of perfect soundness vouchsafed to a nation wearied by disaster and torn by internal strife. Such "salvation," such deliverance, Messiah was to bring. But, on the other hand, the word, as St. Peter uses it, is already being transplanted into the spiritual sphere; already it speaks of blessings corresponding to the needs of every part of our nature, the full sum of all the divine activities and gifts which meet the case of sinful man.

There are two designations of our Lord in St. Peter's speeches which claim particular notice.

(1) The Lord Jesus is "the Holy and

---

[1] I have given the eighth *Benediction* in the fullest form. In the "Babylonian" recension of the *Benedictions* (Dalman, *Die Worte Jesu*, p. 302) it is somewhat briefer. In the "Palestinian" recension (*ib*. p. 300) it runs thus: "Heal us, Jehovah our God, from the trouble of our heart; and sorrow and sighing remove from us, and bring healing for our strokes. Blessed art Thou, even He that healeth the diseased of His people Israel."

Righteous One" (iii. 14; comp. iv. 27, 30). In the speech of St. Stephen and in the message of Ananias, the Hebrew disciple at Damascus, He is "the Righteous One" (vii. 52, xxii. 14). Nowhere else in the Acts or in the New Testament are these terms thus used. Both these conceptions of the Messianic character—holiness and righteousness—are drawn from the very fountain of the Messianic idea. Jehovah is holy and righteous. Israel is holy and righteous. He therefore who is the vicegerent of Jehovah and the flower and consummation of Israel must in the highest degree possess these endowments. And as a matter of fact both these characteristics have a prominent place in the pre-Christian pictures of Messiah—"He is free from sin" (Pss. Sol. xvii. 41); "He is a righteous king and taught of God" (*ib.* 35). In the *Book of Enoch* "the Righteous One" is, as in the Acts, a title of the Messiah. He is "the Righteous and Elect One" (liii. 6); "The Righteous One shall appear before the eyes of the elect righteous ones" (xxxviii. 2); "This is the Son of Man who hath righteousness, with whom dwelleth righteousness" (xlvi. 3). In later Jewish writings and prayers such phrases as "our righteous Messiah," "Thy righteous Messiah," are not uncommon (Dalman, *Die Worte Jesu*, p. 241). The peculiar combination found in the Acts, "holy and righteous," does not, so far as I have observed, occur elsewhere as a description of the Messiah Himself; but in *Enoch* "the righteous and holy ones" is in several passages a designation of the Messianic *people* (xxxviii. 5, xlviii. 1, 7, li. 2). It is only when the close relation between the Messiah and the Messianic people, which is so clearly implied in *Enoch*, and which was explicitly recognised in later Jewish literature (see the Midrash quoted in Edersheim's *Life and Times of Jesus the Messiah*, ii. p. 716), is borne in mind that the full significance of St. Peter's words appears. By their deliberate rejection of the "Holy and Righteous" Messiah, and their deliberate approval of a "murderer" as the man of their choice, the people repudiated their position as the Messianic nation, and passed over into the ranks of the ungodly and sinful.

As before, so here also, we notice that the Jewish words and the Jewish conceptions were ready for the highest Christian uses. We remember St. Paul's teaching about "the righteousness of Christ." We remember how St. John, who, as he was dreaming youthful dreams of the glories of Messiah's coming, was pointed by the Forerunner to "the Lamb of God," long after, when he had lived on into the new age, took up the familiar Messianic titles and applied them to the Lord in His heavenly ministry—"We have an Advocate with the Father, Jesus Christ the Righteous One"; "Ye have an anointing from the Holy One" (1 John ii. 1, 20). We have then, on the one hand, the Jewish application of the terms *Righteous* and *Holy* to the Messiah and the Messianic people, and, on the other hand, St. John's use of these words in relation to the Lord in Heaven. St. John's language seems to imply an intermediate stage in the history of these Christological expressions; an application of them, that is, to the historical Christ such as we find in the Petrine speeches of the Acts.

(2) If these words describe Messiah's character, another phrase expresses his relation

to God—"the Servant," "the Servant of the Lord." The title occurs four times in the Acts, twice in the prayer of the Apostles in chapter iv. (iii. 13, 26, iv. 27, 30). It is, of course, derived from a series of passages in the deutero-Isaiah, where it primarily points to the people of Israel personified in its Godward relations.[1] According to the principle referred to above, based on the quasi-identification of the Messiah with the Messianic people, the title of the idealized Israel was transferred to the idealized ruler. In later Jewish exegesis this personal interpretation of the prophet's words was the current one. According to the Targum on Is. xliii. 10 (Dalman, *ib.* p. 227; Edersheim, *Life and Times*, ii. p. 726), Jehovah speaks through the prophet to "my servant the Messiah." And the use of this title in Apostolic days is certified by its occurrence in the *Apocalypse of Baruch* (lxx. 9): "Whosoever escapes . . . will be delivered into the hands of my servant Messiah." It was then in accordance with the mode of speech prevalent among the Jews that

---

[1] Driver, *Isaiah, His Life and Times*, pp. 175 ff.; Kirkpatrick, *The Doctrine of the Prophets*, pp. 381 ff.

St. Peter should call Him whose Messiahship he proclaimed "the Servant."[1] But here an important consideration comes in. The Hebrew word (עֶבֶד), used by the prophet in this series of passages, means, and can only mean, *servant*. The Greek word (παῖς), which the LXX. translator chose as the equivalent in most of these passages, is ambiguous; it may mean *servant* or it may mean *son*. Hence a Hellenistic Jew, reading Isaiah in the LXX., might well interpret these prophecies as dealing with, or as addressed to, Jehovah's *son*. That this interpretation was as a fact current among Greek-speaking Jews appears from two considerations. In the first place we appeal to the Alexandrian Book of Wisdom. Here (ii. 12-20) a description is given of the "righteous man." His persecutors taunt him with his presumption—"He nameth himself παῖς Κυρίου."

---

[1] That the word παῖς in the Acts means *servant*, not *son* (*child*), seems clear (1) from the juxtaposition in the Apostolic prayer (iv. 24-30) of the phrases τὸν ἅγιον παῖδά σου Ἰησοῦν and τοῦ ἁγίου παιδός σου Ἰησοῦ and the phrase Δαυεὶδ παιδός σου; the latter phrase, the unambiguous Hebrew original of which is common in Jewish prayers (see p. 139), must mean "thy *servant* David" (comp. Luke i. 54, 69); (2) from the fact that there is not in the context of any of the four passages any such word as *father*, *beloved* (see p. 140).

"He vaunteth that God is his Father." "Let us see if his words be true, and let us try what shall befall in the ending of his life. For if the righteous man is *God's son*, he will uphold him." In this passage the whole connexion of thought makes it plain that the writer understood παῖς Κυρίου as meaning "the Lord's *son*." Again, in Matt. xii. 18 ff. we have a Greek translation of Is. xlii. 1 ff. (differing from the LXX. and not without points of similarity to the rendering of Theodotion) in which the fact that ὁ ἀγαπητός μου is parallel to ὁ παῖς μου seems to make it clear that παῖς must be taken as meaning *son*. This conclusion is confirmed when we turn to the accounts of the Baptism and of the Transfiguration of our Lord (Matt. iii. 17, Mark i. 11, Luke iii. 22; Matt. xvii. 5, Mark ix. 7, Luke ix. 35). On both occasions the voice from heaven greets our Saviour as "my Son" (ὁ υἱός μου). But it is clear that the Greek representation of the divine words, which lies behind the Synoptists' report, is based on that revised Greek version of Is. xlii. 1—probably a Palestinian version—to which reference has just been made.

From these facts it seems to be a necessary

inference that, while the Jews who could read the Hebrew text or who used an Aramaic paraphrase invariably understood the prophet to be referring to "the *servant* of the Lord," many Hellenistic Jews took his words as applying to "the *son* of the Lord."

From the different interpretations of the prophet's phrase current among the Hebrews and among the Hellenists, we pass to the consideration of its use in the early Christian Church. The word *servant* is not uncommon in Jewish prayers in reference to David, the type of the Messianic king—"The sprout of David Thy servant cause to flourish" (*Benediction* xv.). "Let all who trust in Thee rejoice . . . in the sprout of David Thy servant" (*Habinenu*[1]). "May our remembrance rise and come and be accepted before Thee, and the remembrance of our Fathers, and the remembrance of Messiah the son of David, Thy servant" (*Authorised Daily Prayer Book*,

[1] The word *Habinenu* ("cause us to understand") is the first word, and the name, of a prayer which is a kind of summary of the *Eighteen Benedictions* (Dalman, *Die Worte Jesu*, p. 304). The above phrase—*David Thy servant*—has a place both in the Palestinian and in the Babylonian recension of the *Habinenu*. It is found in the Babylonian, but not in the Palestinian, recension of *Benediction* xv.

p. 241). With these Messianic and liturgical associations, probably through the medium of the Hellenistic synagogues, the word, represented by its Greek equivalent παῖς, passed over into the liturgical vocabulary of the Christian Church. It is found, in application to our Lord, in a series of prayers or liturgical passages in sub-Apostolic and early Christian literature (Clem. 59 [thrice]; *Mart. Polyc.* 14; *Acta Theclae* 24; comp. *Ep. Diog.* 8). But now the Christian consciousness, accustomed to the devout contemplation of the Lord's divine nature and quickened by the controversies with the Ebionites, shrank from speaking of Him as "servant," and hence jealously guarded the interpretation of the word by the addition of the unambiguous epithets "beloved," "only begotten." The only passages in early Christian literature (apart from the Acts) where the word παῖς is used of our Lord in the sense of *servant* are two Eucharistic prayers in the *Didaché*, clearly of extreme antiquity and based on Jewish prayers—"We thank Thee for the holy vine of David Thy *servant*, which Thou didst make known to us by Jesus Thy *servant*."

Thus the use of the pre-Christian Messianic title *the Servant* is most primitive. It carries us back into the days when the vocabulary of the Church was in the earliest stage of its history.

II. We pass on now to consider the witness borne in the Petrine speeches to the historical events of our Lord's life on earth.

The Lord's ministry fills but a little space in the speeches which belong to the early period of the history. It was well known to St. Peter's hearers at Jerusalem, and it was overshadowed by more recent events. In the address of St. Peter to the household at Cæsarea, delivered at a much later time, it is noteworthy that greater stress is laid on the history of our Lord before the Passion (x. 36-39). Here the Apostle refers to the Baptism as the inauguration of the Lord's Messiahship: "God anointed Him with the Holy Ghost and with power" (comp. iv. 27). The words are an echo of the prophecy of Isaiah (lxi. 1), which the Lord claimed for Himself in the synagogue at Nazareth (Luke iv. 17 ff.). From another point of view they have a remarkable parallel in the picture of the Messiah presented to us in the *Psalms of Solomon* (xvii. 42)—"God made him mighty by the Holy Spirit" (ὁ θεὸς κατηργάσατο αὐτὸν δυνατὸν ἐν πνεύματι ἁγίῳ). On the day of Pentecost one and only one side of the Lord's ministry is touched upon by St. Peter. "Jesus the Nazarene, a man proved to be from God to you" (ἀποδεδειγμένον ἀπὸ τοῦ θεοῦ εἰς ὑμᾶς δυνάμεσιν κ.τ.λ.)—a messenger from God to Israel (so I venture to think the words must be understood; comp. John iii. 2) —"by mighty works and wonders and signs, which God did by Him in the midst of you, even as ye yourselves know" (ii. 22). These words, together with the briefer allusion in x. 38, are the only references in the New Testament, outside the Gospels, to the Lord's ministry of miracles. Miracles are like special providences and (as we call them) remarkable answers to prayer. Such experiences bring assurance—a deep and happy assurance—of the watchful and loving care of God to him to whom they are vouchsafed. But the assurance in its fulness is for himself alone. He cannot communicate it to a stranger. Let him tell his tale to a fellow-Christian wearily plodding on along a dull road of daily duty and care, unvisited by any such bright angels from heaven, to him it will be a tale with little or no living force; nay, though he does not question the providence of God, this story, which no experience of his own enables him to realize, calls into activity the sceptical instinct within him, and he becomes alive to possibilities of misinterpretation and exaggeration. He is no unbeliever; but this special piece of evidence finds no response within himself. The appeal made just in this one speech to those who had themselves seen the Lord's wonderful works, taken in connexion with the silence of the New Testament writers elsewhere, is full of meaning. The naturalness of it here is emphasized by the very absence of anything like it elsewhere.

St. Peter's words here as to our Lord's miracles are in remarkable harmony with the historical and doctrinal teaching of St. John's Gospel. They refer to a ministry of miracles in Judæa, which is not recorded by St. Luke or by the other Synoptists, but which is a special theme of St. John. Again, the interpretation of the Lord's miracles, briefly and very simply set forth in the Petrine speech, is that which is characteristic of the discourses in St. John. They not only answered to the popular Messianic expectation (John vii. 31; comp. Joseph. *Antiq.* xx. viii. 6), but they were proofs, easy of discernment, of a divine commission and a divine presence (Acts ii. 22, x. 38). "We know that thou art a teacher come from God: for no man can do these signs that thou doest, except God be with him"; "The very works that I do bear witness of me, that the Father hath sent me"; "The Father abiding in me doeth his works" (John iii. 2, v. 36, xiv. 10). The miracles of Jesus the Nazarene bore witness to those who saw them that He came from God, and that God was with Him.

The sufferings and death of Jesus of Nazareth naturally occupy in these speeches a far larger space than the ministry. We have already seen how closely the speeches of St. Peter keep to the language of the Messianic hope and of the popular Messianic conceptions. But in the sufferings of an alleged Messiah there was something new—shamefully, audaciously new. Within the compass of national expectation there was no room for a crucified Messiah. Three centuries of national sorrows had to elapse before the idea of a suffering Messiah became familiar to Jewish thought. If the Jewish author of the *Second Book of Esdras* speaks of the death of Messiah, it has no special significance attaching to it. The writer, in the deep melancholy of his views of human life and human destiny, conceives of the world as at last overwhelmed by a universal winter in which all life withers and passes away—"After these years shall my son Christ die, and all that have the breath of life. And the world shall be turned into the old silence seven days, like as in the first beginning: so that no man shall remain" (vii. 29 f.). But in general the death of Messiah was not spoken of in Jewish anticipations of the coming age of triumph any more than the certainty of his death would be a favourite theme in the panegyric of any great national hero. It was not the fact that Jesus

Christ died, but that He died as He did, that seemed to give the lie to the Messianic claims which His followers made for Him.

As to the sufferings of Jesus of Nazareth St. Peter is represented as insisting on two points.

(*a*) Jewish thought, at least in some of its forms, dwelt on the predestination of Messiah. The thought finds remarkable expression in the *Book of Enoch* : " And before the sun and the signs were created, before the stars of the heaven were made, [the] name [of the Son of Man] was named before the Lord of Spirits" (xlviii. 3 ; comp. 2 Esdras vii. 28, xii. 32, xiii. 26, 52 ; Pss. Sol. xvii. 23). In the speeches of the Acts the idea of Messiah's predestination is emphasized, but it is emphasized in regard to the sufferings of Jesus. *They* are brought within the folds of the divine will for His Anointed One ; *they* also had a sure place in the working out through Him of the divine purpose. On the human side there were the ignorance and the hatred of rulers and of people. On the divine side there was "the determinate counsel and foreknowledge of God" (ii. 23). The enemies of Jesus did "whatsoever thy hand and thy counsel foreordained to come to pass" (iv. 28). The crucifixion of Jesus was no chance victory snatched by the Jewish rulers. "Suffering" was a necessary element in the divinely-ordered service of Messiah (comp. Luke xxiv. 26).

(β) And, in the second place, St. Peter, according to the representation of his words in the Acts, anticipates the worst which the Lord's enemies could say of the humiliation and the religious ignominy involved in the sufferings endured by Jesus. With a few allusive words he recalls to his hearers on the day of Pentecost what had happened at the last Passover feast. I doubt whether any other Greek sentence could describe so vividly and from so many sides the outward sufferings of the Saviour — τοῦτον . . . ἔκδοτον διὰ χειρὸς ἀνόμων προσπήξαντες ἀνείλατε (ii. 23). The words bring before our minds the horror of abandonment by man and by God to the pitilessness of enemies; the degradation involved in the instruments of the execution—"sinners of the Gentiles"; the inhuman simplicity of the mode of death. But beyond all the other sufferings there was one mystery of humiliation. There is an explicit reference to it in the speech before the Sanhedrin—"whom ye slew, hanging him on a tree" (v. 30; comp. x. 39, xiii. 29). The allusion is to two sentences in a well-known passage of the Law (Deut. xxi. 22 f.), a passage which has influenced the language of the New Testament in more passages than we are wont to think : " If ... thou hang [a man] on a tree . . . he that is hanged is the curse of God." In two ways the words "hanging him on a tree," recalling, as they could not but do, their context in Deuteronomy, were relevant. In the first place, on a loose interpretation of the Hebrew words, "he that is hanged is the curse of God," was based the later Jewish law for the punishment of blasphemy, as it is recorded by Josephus (*Antiq.* IV. viii. 6): "Let him that blasphemeth God be stoned and hang all day, and let him be buried with dishonour and in obscurity." The High Priest, before whom St. Peter is represented as speaking, had condemned Jesus of Nazareth as a blasphemer. As a blasphemer the manner of His death—"hanged upon a tree"—had in Jewish eyes proclaimed Him before God and man. Again, according to the natural, and, as it appears, the current interpretation of the words of Deuteronomy, an interpretation adopted by the LXX., he that was "hanged upon a tree" was "accursed by God." To a Jew then the cross was infinitely more than an earthly punishment of unutterable suffering and shame; it was a revelation that on the crucified there rested the extreme malediction of the wrath of God. The idea was no theological refinement. It could not but be present to the mind of every Jew who knew the Law. Within a few years, as we learn from St. Paul (1 Cor. xii. 3), it was formulated in a creed of unbelief—ἀνάθεμα Ἰησοῦς. It found expression in the name by which in later days the Lord was known among the Jews—הַתָּלוּי, "the hanged one." The Sanhedrin, before whom St. Peter is represented as speaking, regarded Jesus the Nazarene as a blasphemer and as one accursed by God. Behind the phrase put into the mouth of the Apostle there lies a controversial background which we can restore only when we carefully piece together scattered indications of Jewish thought.

"Whom ye slew, hanging him on a tree." Here was a public, an impressive, a final attestation what Jesus of Nazareth was in the sight of God. Here was an end. "He trusted on God; let him deliver him now, if he desireth him; for he said, I am the Son of God" (Matt. xxvii. 43). But there had been no deliverance. God had been silent. There could be but one conclusion, one certain conclusion, drawn from the very words of Scripture—$\dot{a}νάθεμα$ '$Ιησοῦς$. An end? No deliverance? "Accursed"? Nay, "whom ye crucified, whom God raised from the dead" (iv. 10). "Ye . . . killed the Prince of life; whom God raised from the dead" (iii. 15). "Him . . . ye by the hand of lawless men did crucify and slay: whom God raised up" (ii. 23 f.). The Resurrection, the immediate act of God, was the divine reversal of Israel's rejection, the divine answer to Israel's blasphemy. Jesus, raised by the Father from the dead, could not be "accursed."

But the Resurrection from the Dead was a preface to the Exaltation. "Being therefore by the right hand of God exalted, and having received of the Father the promise of the Holy Ghost, he hath poured forth this, which ye see and hear. For David ascended not into the heavens" (ii. 33 f.). Here again there seems to be lurking in the background a step in the unfolding of the Lord's glories which is only hinted at in St. Luke's summary of the speech. What calls for the caution, "For David ascended not into the heavens"? Why this "For"? Surely some words of a psalm about "ascension" or "exaltation" had been quoted, which *might* have been applied by a superficial reader to the ancient king. And when to the consideration of the sequence of thought we add a consideration of the language—ὑψωθείς, ἀνέβη, λαβών (ii. 33 f.)—we are led to conjecture that the words of the great psalm of triumph—"Thou hast ascended on high . . . Thou hast received gifts" (ἀναβὰς εἰς ὕψος . . . ἔλαβες δόματα, Ps. lxvii. [lxviii.] 19)—had in reality been adduced by St. Peter to express, or to confirm, his witness to the Lord's Ascension. And if this view be correct, then we are able to point back to something implied, but not explicitly expressed, in the speech as we have it—a relic of an authority fuller than St. Luke's obviously abbreviated version of St. Peter's words, fuller and more original.

"Raised from the dead," "by the right hand of God exalted," "glorified,"—such are the phrases used in these speeches to express the facts of the history and the different aspects of the Lord's majesty. Two questions at once arise. How is it said that the facts are attested? To what conclusion as to the Lord's Person are they taken as pointing?

(*a*) How were the hearers of the Apostolic words to know that the divine reversal of Israel's rejection was a fact? To what evidence is the speaker represented as making his appeal? The story of the Cross was notorious; no one denied it. What of the Resurrection and Ascension? The different elements of the answer to this necessary question are scattered throughout the speeches. The assurance of the Resurrection and the Ascension was to be found in the prophetic words of Scripture—the words which were universally regarded as the words of David, but which in the magnificence of their hope could not be true of him whose sepulchre was in the midst of his people. It was to be found in the actual experience of those particular Israelites on the day of Pentecost—"this which ye see and hear" (ii. 33). It was to be found in the present beneficent activity of Jesus of Nazareth—in the miracle wrought in His name: He is active; therefore He lives. It was to be found in the personal testimony of the Apostles themselves to "the things which they had seen and heard" (iv. 20). It was to be found lastly in the inner witness of the Spirit—"we are witnesses of these things; and so is the Holy Ghost" (v. 32)—the Spirit who revealed the fitness of the Resurrection and its harmony with the divine purpose as partially shadowed forth in the words of Scripture. Such are the evidences of his Gospel which the Apostle is represented as pleading. They are not set forth systematically; but when we reflect on them together, the appeal is absolutely congruous with the supposed situation, and it would be hard to add another to this series of testimonies.

(*b*) What is the inference which, in St. Luke's record of his words, St. Peter draws for his brother Israelites from these facts? It is contained in the solemn charge with which the Pentecostal sermon closes: "Let all the house of Israel know therefore assuredly, that God hath made him both Lord and Christ, this Jesus whom ye crucified" (ii. 36). It is not, of course, that Messiahship and Lordship first then belonged to Jesus Christ when the shame of the cross was obliterated. But then they were proved by God's act to be His true prerogatives. He was then set forth finally as Messiah and as Lord.

It is at this point more than at any other that we desire a decisive answer to the question, What was the original language of the speech? If the Apostle used Aramaic, then it seems certain from the usage of that language that the term he used was not *Lord*, but *our Lord*[1] —"God hath made him our Lord"; thus the stringency of the title *Lord* used absolutely is to some extent, at least in appearance,

[1] Dalman, *Die Worte Jesu*, p. 268.

softened.¹ And further, on this supposition as to the original language, the particular word used must almost certainly have been *Marana* or *Maran*, which we know from the *Maranatha*² preserved by St. Paul (1 Cor. xvi. 22) and in the *Didachê* (x. ; comp. *Apost. Constit.* vii. 26) to have been in early use among Jewish Christians as a designation of Jesus Christ.³

But, in truth, as to the broad significance of these words, in which the Apostle is represented as summing up his witness to the Person of Jesus, it matters little whether he spoke in

---

¹ But compare Acts x. 36 (οὗτός ἐστιν πάντων κύριος), Rom. x. 12, Eph. iv. 10.

² The probable meaning of *Maranatha* (i.e. *Marana-tha*) is, "Our Lord come" (see Thayer's article in Hastings' *Dict. of the Bible*, iii. p. 241). Compare Apoc. xxii. 20 (ἔρχου Κύριε Ἰησοῦ) and the *Amen bo* (Amen, come) found in a Jewish prayer (Taylor, *The Teaching of the Twelve Apostles*, pp. 77 ff.).

³ The only other Aramaic word which could have been used is Rabbonana (Ribbonana), *i.e.* our Rabbon. Compare ῥαββουνεί (*i.e.* my Rabbon : Mark x. 51, John xx. 16). But Rabboni cannot have been essentially different from Rabbi (Dalman, *Die Worte Jesu*, p. 279); and St. John's interpretation (ὃ λέγεται Διδάσκαλε) shews that the disciples connected the title with conceptions which would be wholly alien to the context in Acts ii. 36. On the other hand, Mari would certainly be the word which would naturally represent the "my Lord" of Psalm cx. 1 (so *Evang. Hierosol.* in Matt. xxii. 44), quoted by St. Peter in the immediately preceding context.

Aramaic or in Greek. These titles—Christ, Lord—were no new inventions. The designation *Lord*, as well as Christ, had a history in the past. In the Old Testament the terms "the Anointed," "King," "Lord" ("my Lord," that is, and the like) were closely related together (comp. *e.g.* 1 Sam. xxiv. 6, 8, 10). Later Jewish literature shews that the word *lord* (*mār*) was used in a great variety of applications—of earthly masters, of the High Priest, of the King, of Messiah, of God Himself.[1] Turning from the Hebrew and Aramaic, we note that in the LXX., over and above the "my Lord" and the like representing the Hebrew, we once, through a mistaken translation, have the term χριστὸς κύριος used of the earthly king (Lam. iv. 20). Once again, in the *Psalms of Solomon* (xvii. 36) the king of the restored and purified Israel is χριστὸς κύριος (comp. Luke ii. 11). Both in the Aramaic then and in the Greek the term *Lord* is a form of reverential address or designation, the exact shade of meaning being determined by the context. And here the context—the context

---

[1] Dalman, *Die Worte Jesu*, pp. 147 f., 266 ff.

of history and the context of Scripture, "Jehovah said to my Lord, Sit thou on my right hand," raises the ancient title above the sphere of the human and the earthly. If the title *Messiah* chiefly emphasizes the divine appointment to kingship, the title *Lord* expresses majesty and sovereignty: and that majesty is seated on the right hand of God; from the right hand of God that sovereignty is exercised. The first Christian sermon culminates in the first Christian creed, Κύριος Ἰησοῦς, Κύριος Ἰησοῦς Χριστός (1 Cor. xii. 3, Rom. x. 9; Phil. ii. 11).

Thus the immemorial language of reverence, reaching back to the loyal dutifulness which surrounded and ennobled the throne of David, language not without the consecration of religious use, is now raised to a new and loftier significance. It expresses a sovereignty which belongs not to an earthly monarch but to a heavenly king. When such language became habitual, when adoration and worship were seen to be its necessary corollary, then the belief of the Catholic Church as to the Person of Christ had taken a firm hold on the hearts and consciences of His disciples. In this language, and in the facts of the Resurrection and the Exaltation which called it forth, there lay the premises from which there was inevitably drawn the inference — the certain and awful inference—of the Divinity of Jesus Christ. But this conclusion is not as yet asserted. The divine nature of Jesus the Messiah is not as yet explicitly confessed. For the present the terms in which the Apostle describes his Master's glory and the issues of his Master's work are borrowed from the language of the Messianic hope. The predestination of Jesus the Messiah is spoken of (ii. 23, iii. 18; comp. iv. 28), but His pre-existence is not affirmed, nor is anything said of His unique relation to the Father. The Lord's death is not brought into connexion with the conception of atonement, nor with the problem of justification. There is no allusion to the moral and spiritual power of the Resurrection, or to the sanctifying influence of the Holy Spirit. If we compare St. Peter's speeches with any one of the Apostolic Epistles (except that of St. James, which deals almost wholly with matters of conduct), we see the wide difference between a matured apprehension and exposition of the Christian facts in their universal and absolute significance, and, on the other hand, an immediate interpretation of them addressed to Jews at Jerusalem, many of whom had cried, "Crucify Him," and had watched the death "upon the tree" of Jesus of Nazareth.

The more carefully we study the Petrine speeches of the Acts, their language and their thought, the deeper becomes our conviction that there is a real harmony between them and the alleged occasions of their utterance; and that, both from a literary and from a theological standpoint, they cannot be the invention of the Gentile author of the Book—familiar, as he certainly was, with the teaching of St. Paul, and writing when the peculiar circumstances and the phases of thought which they presuppose had long passed away.

And here I should close, were it not right that I should refer, however inadequately, to one subject which is prominent in our minds to-day [1]—prominent even at a time when our hearts, as the hearts of all Englishmen, are deeply moved by anxiety for our beloved Queen, whom may God in His mercy still preserve to us; whom may God ever sustain, in life and in death, with the comfort of His presence and His love.

The mystery and the pathos of human life are seen by us in one of their most impressive forms when a place of signal honour and of great responsibility is suddenly left vacant, and its occupant is called away from a strenuous and buoyant maturity, unsaddened by any failure, and, till just the last, untouched by the withering hand of decay; when the triumphant progress from strength to strength is in a moment arrested; and the man with whom the world has not learned to associate the idea of weariness rests from his labours.

Few men in his generation had grasped life so firmly and at so many points as Bishop Creighton. A brilliant teacher in the sister University, he was called from the busy leisure

[1] Dr. Creighton, Bishop of London, died on Monday, January 14.

of a country vicarage to be the first occupant of the Chair of Ecclesiastical History among ourselves. How he justified the choice, how he served the University who welcomed him as her adopted son, I need not remind you. Even those whose studies lay in other spheres of knowledge, and who did not come under his immediate influence, recognised that Cambridge had gained for a time the presence of a strong and striking personality, and the loyal service of an historian of European reputation. Soon —too soon, we perhaps think—the call came to him to take his place among the fathers and chief pastors of the National Church; and later the summons—recognised by him, it seems, less as an advance to fresh honours than as a challenge to unknown self-sacrifice—to gird himself for the almost superhuman task of ruling and guiding the church of the metropolis.

With Bishop Creighton, as with Bishop Lightfoot, the gifts of the student, enlarged by a wide experience of life, and disciplined by the serious work of the teacher and by the historian's minute and laborious search after truth, were transfigured into the spirit of counsel and the wise activities of the ecclesiastical statesman. The final endeavour of his episcopate was, as you know, to help men to penetrate beneath the fleeting fashions of controversy to the fundamental truths which are knit together in the doctrine of the Eucharist. Sometimes the last act of a great man interprets to those who remain a complex character and gives something of unity to the manifold aims and currents of the life.

It is impossible not to compare the late Bishop of London with a great Dean of his own Cathedral, whom some here may still remember, and whose venerable and commanding presence lives among the memories of my boyhood. The resemblances and the contrasts between the two men are alike significant. Dean Milman, after the conflicts of earlier years, reached a haven whence, as a calm spectator, he could watch the strife of tongues and the feverish activities of a new age with its new needs and new methods. Bishop Creighton, from a life of scholarly quiet, passed (with but a brief interval) to that place in the English Church where there can be no pause, no rest, no refuge from the swarm of stinging anxieties, no freedom from responsible decisions, no cessation of the remorseless turmoil of strife and debate. But there are substantial similarities between the two lives. Both were marked men among their contemporaries at Oxford. Both, as historians, took a foremost place among the English men of letters of their day. Both dedicated their powers to the epic of Latin Christianity. Both were acknowledged as being in a pre-eminent degree links between the faith and the theology and the work of the Church and the world of literature and art and science. Both rest in the Cathedral in which they were chief ministers—the one who lived to be revered, to use Dean Stanley's word, as "the wise old man"; the other who "in a short time fulfilled a long time."

The lesson of such a life as we commemorate to-day is plain and simple—we can all understand it; we all need it—the dedication of gifts of character and ability (be they great or small), the use of such opportunities of service as our Father in Heaven is pleased to give us, for the glory of God and the benefit of His Holy Church.

LECTURE IV

Δαυεὶδ μὲν γὰρ ἰδίᾳ γενεᾷ ὑπηρετήσας τῇ τοῦ θεοῦ βουλῇ
ἐκοιμήθη καὶ προσετέθη πρὸς τοὺς πατέρας αὐτοῦ.

3RD SUNDAY AFTER EPIPHANY,
January 27, 1901.

IV

"David, after he had served his own generation, by the counsel of God fell on sleep, and was laid unto his fathers."—ACTS xiii. 36.[1]

No one, I think, who ever held the office in virtue of which it is my duty to speak to you to-day has had a task so sad and so heavy as that which has been mine last Sunday and this Sunday. A week ago it was hard, under the dark shadow of an impending sorrow, to claim your attention to the details of a subject of Biblical criticism. To-day, when one only thought fills the mind of all, it is harder still. I ask your forbearance, and I think that I shall not ask it in vain, while I bring before you first of all some portion of

[1] Part of the Second Lesson at Evensong on Tuesday, 22nd January, the day on which Queen Victoria died.

Only the earlier portion of this lecture and the part which deals with Acts xiii. 15-41 were actually delivered.

that special subject which still remains for our consideration—the witness of St. Paul.

St. Paul's activity extended over the whole of the wide domain of the Church's life. He sowed the seed of the word. He tended the rising plant. He controlled the work of his fellow-husbandmen, and brought it to pass that the spiritual plants were no isolated growths, but together became well-ordered "gardens of the Lord." In other words, the Apostle was an evangelist, a pastor, a ruler. It is in the two latter aspects of his missionary work that we know him in his Epistles. His writings are an abiding source of guidance to the Christian Church, because in them he spoke to men who had already become Christian, and who were in the same lists in which we struggle now. We have indeed in the Epistles glimpses of the earlier stages of his work; we learn something of his methods, still more of the spirit which inspired those methods. We cannot break up a living ministry into independent sections. Yet it remains true that in the

Epistles it is not so much Paul the Herald as Paul the spiritual Counsellor and Paul the Ruler of Churches who is presented to us. For materials with which to complete the portrait we must turn, if it be veracious, to the Book of the Acts. There we have what purports to be a representation of the Apostle as a sower of the spiritual seed—nay, as the husbandman whose supreme office it was to be the first to break up the fallow ground of the heathen world.

Our task, then, in this final lecture is to examine the witness of St. Paul as it is presented to us in the Acts. In this investigation we must always keep in view these three questions:

(1) What is the relation of the Pauline to the Petrine speeches in the Acts? Though it is granted that all alike bear the marks of having passed through the same editor's hand, is there, nevertheless, a real and substantial difference between the two series in regard to doctrine, and, though necessarily in a less conspicuous degree, in regard to diction?

(2) What is the relation of the Pauline speeches to the Pauline Epistles? On the one

hand, are the speeches independent, *i.e.* no mere literary copies of the Epistles? On the other, can we trace, working behind the speeches, the same mind which conceived the thoughts and fashioned the language of the Epistles—the same mind, but dealing in the speeches (except in the one addressed to the Elders of Ephesus) with situations and with subjects which could have little or no place in the Epistles?

(3) What is the mutual relation between the Pauline speeches? Does their congruity with their several alleged occasions refute the theory that they are the invention of the writer of the Book?

One not unimportant point in such a comparison between the Pauline letters and the Pauline speeches, it will from the nature of the case be impossible to treat with any degree of thoroughness—I mean coincidences in language. All the speeches afford such parallels, but not all in the same proportion. The address to the Elders of Ephesus is richest in this respect; and this is that one among the Pauline speeches, at which, according to our working hypothesis, St. Luke himself was present, and which we saw (p. 112) reasons for thinking to be based on notes of St. Paul's words taken at the time. Yet even here such coincidences are not ostentatiously introduced, nor are they characterized by mechanical precision. When we compare the Epistles and the speeches, we discover not identity of phraseology, but resemblance of language—a resemblance which often lies beneath the surface of the words.

The occasions during his long missionary career on which St. Paul spoke as an evangelist and as a pastor must have been numberless. In the Acts we have specimens of his addresses drawn from the several periods of his active work, and representing its different elements. The selection is made so skilfully,—it is so thoroughly in harmony with what the Epistles reveal of the Apostle's mind,—that the supposition that he himself was St. Luke's authority for these speeches (p. 120) is confirmed. The Jew had the priority in St. Paul's order of evangelization (Rom. i. 16; comp. ii. 9). Of the Apostle's pleading with his own fellow-countrymen we have examples in the brief but important notice of his work at Damascus, in the speech at Antioch of Pisidia (during the first missionary journey), and in his last appeal to the Jews at Rome. Again, the "Apostle of the Gentiles" describes himself as "a debtor both to Greeks and to Barbarians, both to the wise and to the foolish" (Rom. i. 14). Accordingly, of his "hortatory discourses" (to use Clement's phrase)—his first call to the Gentiles to come forth from the cave in which the realities of life could not be recognized in the false and fleeting shadows which mocked them—we have specimens in the speech addressed to the simple folk of Lystra, and, on the other hand, in the discourse to which a little group of Athenians is represented as listening on the Areopagus. Lastly, since in the spiritual husbandry of the Apostle there was watering as well as sowing, the Book includes one other representative utterance—the pastoral speech at Miletus.

1. We turn first to St. Paul's witness to Israel.

Among the Epistles of St. Paul we have none analogous to the Epistle of St. James and the Epistle to the Hebrews—letters addressed, as it appears, to purely Jewish communities. In the churches founded by St. Paul the Jewish Christians were united with the Gentile Christians in the one brotherhood. In the Christian assemblies the Apostle, doubtless, from time to time turned and addressed himself now to the Jews, now to the Gentiles, among his hearers. Of these prophetic utterances in the Church we probably have echoes in the Epistles. Here we have a natural explanation of the fact that in a single Epistle we find one passage in which St. Paul appears to speak to Jewish converts, and another passage in which he appeals to Gentile converts.[1] Though, therefore, there are in the Epistles of St. Paul exhortations and arguments which are specially addressed to Jews, it yet remains true that in the Apostle's writings we have no distinct and detailed example of the way in which he presented the Gospel to his own fellow-countrymen. The Epistles, therefore, supply no model on which a romancer could construct a Pauline sermon to

---

[1] *E.g.* Rom. ii. 17 ff., iii. 9, iv. 1 (Jews); xi. 13 (Gentiles): 1 Cor. x. 1 (Jews); xii. 2 (Gentiles).

Jews. We have to inquire whether the record in the Acts of St. Paul's teaching addressed to Jews can be shewn to be intrinsically probable. If it stands the test of such a scrutiny, we are justified in regarding the Book, in respect of this important subject, as complementary to the Epistles, and as, in this respect also, bearing witness to its own veracity.

The beginning of St. Paul's ministry to Israel was the immediate sequel of his conversion. "Straightway in the synagogues he proclaimed Jesus, that he is the Son of God." The surprise and anger of the Jews, the historian tells us, did but add fuel to the fire of the Apostle's earnestness. "Saul increased the more in strength, and confounded the Jews which dwelt at Damascus, proving that this is the Christ" (ix. 20 ff.). "Jesus is the Son of God," "Jesus is the Christ." What is the relation of these two statements of Saul's doctrine? The question gains emphasis from the fact that this is the only certain occurrence of the title "Son of God" in the Acts.[1] What did that title mean on the lips of the newly called, and

[1] On xx. 28, see below, p. 284.

(from a human point of view) still uninstructed, evangelist? What connexion had it with the current language of that Messianic hope in which the preacher and his hearers alike shared? We must rapidly trace the lines of thought which converge in this sacred title.

(i.) In the Old Testament, Israel, at that crisis of deliverance which in one sense was the beginning of national life, is designated as Jehovah's son: "Thou shalt say unto Pharaoh, Thus saith the Lord, Israel is my son, my firstborn" (Ex. iv. 22; comp. Deut. xxxii. 6, Hos. xi. 1, Jer. xxxi. 9). So in the *Book of Enoch* (lxii. 11) the people are "His children and His elect."

(ii.) The King of the theocracy is Jehovah's son. The thought finds clear expression in the passage which is the foundation of the national Davidic hope: "I will establish the throne of his kingdom for ever. I will be his father, and he shall be my son" (2 Sam. vii. 14). I need not remind you how this conception of the King of Israel is repeated and expanded in the Psalter (Ps. lxxx. 26 f.).

(iii.) On the principle, to which reference

has often been made, that the highest characteristics of the People and of the King are gathered up in the Messiah, we should expect that the Messiah also would be represented as "the Son of God." Nor is this expectation disappointed. In one passage of *Enoch* (cv. 2),[1] and in a series of passages in 2 Esdras (vii. 28 f., xiii. 32, 37, 52, xiv. 9), God is represented as speaking of Messiah as "my Son," "my Son Christ," "I and my Son." Again, the language of the Synoptic Gospels makes it certain that the designation "Son of God" was current as a Messianic title in our Lord's days (*e.g.* Luke iv. 41).[2]

The point then in St. Luke's summary of Saul's preaching at Damascus seems to be this: Saul of Tarsus, who believed with a lifelong intensity of conviction that he himself on earth had seen Jesus in glory, and had heard His voice speaking to him from heaven, isolated and emphasized this aspect of Messiahship; he gave to this Messianic title a new

[1] Dr. Charles (see his note *in loco*) considers the section an interpolation.
[2] Comp. the article on Peter (Simon) in Hastings' *Dictionary of the Bible*, iii. p. 759; Dalman, *Die Worte Jesu*, pp. 224 ff.

and awful significance, as expressing an essential truth about the nature of the glorified Messiah. St. Peter, as we saw in the last lecture (pp. 154 ff.), dwelt upon the exaltation and the sovereignty of Jesus the Messiah. Saul of Tarsus becomes from the first the Theologus of the early Apostolic Church.

The exact language of St. Luke confirms this interpretation of his words. The Messiahship of Jesus was a matter of reasoning and of proof. Scriptures could be adduced and placed side by side. Saul "*proved*" to the Jews "that this is the Christ." The divine Sonship, on the other hand, was a matter rather of immediate conviction and of bold assertion: "He *proclaimed* Jesus, that he is the Son of God."

It is important for us to remark that this historical notice in the Acts is in entire agreement with the language of St. Paul himself, when into one brief sentence he gathers up the history of his conversion and of his communings with himself and with the Spirit of God, who dwelt and spoke within him: "It was the good pleasure of God," he says (Gal. i. 15 f.), "to reveal *his Son* in me."

In the common expectation of the Jews, as we have already seen (p. 145), the death of the Messiah was but the necessary close of life, while in the foreground of the picture there lay the triumph and the splendour of victory and kingship; in Jesus suffering and death were revealed as a necessary and essential part of Messiah's work. In like manner it is now seen and proclaimed with unfaltering clearness that the divine Sonship was not one among many traits of Messiah's character, one casual element in an inheritance derived from royal and national prototypes, a vague and glorious metaphor, but the central fact about Him. In the synagogues of Damascus the antithesis on which the faith of the Catholic Church rests was completed. "Jesus Messiah suffered"—this side of the paradox of the Gospel had been announced from the first. "Jesus Messiah is the Son of God"—this complementary truth is now for the first time (so far as our knowledge goes) clearly and decisively set forth.

Years of quiet preparation and of strenuous

labour elapse before the next occasion from which the writer of the Acts draws another specimen of the Apostle's witness to Israel. Saul the convert has already become Paul the Apostle.

We take up St. Paul's "discourse of exhortation[1]" spoken in the synagogue of the Pisidian Antioch. Before we enter on a discussion of its doctrine, there are two points in the *form* of the speech which demand a brief notice.

(*a*) The speech opens with the words, "The God of this people Israel chose our fathers" (xiii. 17). What is the reference of the expression, "*this* people Israel"? The explanations given by the commentators that the word *this* looks back to the ἄνδρες Ἰσραηλεῖται of the opening address (*v.* 16), or that the speaker accompanied the word by a gesture, pointing to the Israelites before him, seem to me forced and unworthy. I cannot but think that we must look in another direction for the inter-

---

[1] xiii. 15, ἄνδρες ἀδελφοί, εἴ τις ἔστιν ἐν ὑμῖν λόγος παρακλήσεως πρὸς τὸν λαόν, λέγετε. The words λόγος παρακλήσεως are probably a technical phrase used in the synagogues. Comp. Heb. xiii. 22, ἀδελφοί, ἀνέχεσθε τοῦ λόγου τῆς παρακλήσεως: 1 Tim. iv. 13, πρόσεχε τῇ ἀναγνώσει, τῇ παρακλήσει.

pretation. "The reading of the Scriptures" [in the synagogues], says Schürer,[1] "was followed by an edifying discourse or sermon, by which the portion which had been read was explained and applied." Our Lord in the synagogue at Nazareth based the words which He addressed to His fellow-townsmen upon the passage from Isaiah which He had just read (Luke iv. 17 ff.). Is it not natural to suppose that here also the lections from the Law and the Prophets had contained some emphatic reference to the history and privileges of Israel, and that St. Paul followed the common custom of the synagogue, and took up in the opening words of his address the prominent thought of the Scriptures chosen for that Sabbath — "*this* people Israel"? But if this be so, we have once more an indication that behind St. Luke's record there lies a background of facts which in the present instance is revealed only by one allusive word, and that his informant recalled details which have no place in his narrative.

(*b*) Again, when we turn to those passages of the Pauline Epistles where a proof or an

---

[1] *History of the Jewish People*, Eng. Trans., II. ii. p. 82.

illustration of the matter in hand is adduced from the Old Testament, we notice that St. Paul is wont to draw from different parts of the Old Testament, and to quote side by side, texts which are linked together by the common use of some characteristic expression or "catchword"; and further, that he sometimes revises, or adopts a revision of, the Greek of the LXX., in order that he may create or emphasize a verbal resemblance between the passages which he desires to bring together. As instances of this mode of quotation we may quote the repeated ἐπικατάρατος of Gal. iii. 10, 13 ("*Cursed* is every one which continueth not in all things that are written in the book of the law. . . . *Cursed* is every one that hangeth on a tree"), or the repeated νῖκος of 1 Cor. xv. 54 f. ("*Death* is swallowed up in *victory*. O *Death*, where is thy *victory*?").[1] Now this synagogue discourse

---

[1] (*a*) Gal. iii. 10, ἐπικατάρατος πᾶς ὃς οὐκ ἐμμένει κ.τ.λ., is a quotation from Deut. xxvii. 26, ἐπικατάρατος κ.τ.λ.; *v.* 13, ἐπικατάρατος πᾶς ὁ κρεμάμενος κ.τ.λ., from Deut. xxi. 23, κεκαταραμένος ὑπὸ θεοῦ πᾶς κρεμάμενος κ.τ.λ. (*b*) 1 Cor. xv. 54, κατεπόθη ὁ θάνατος εἰς νῖκος, comes from Is. xxv. 8, κατέπιεν ὁ θάνατος ἰσχύσας (Heb. "He hath swallowed up death for ever"); *v.* 55, ποῦ σου, θάνατε, τὸ νῖκος, from Hos. xiii. 14, ποῦ ἡ δίκη σου, θάνατε (Heb. "O death, where are thy plagues?").

is the only passage in the Acts where we have a Pauline argument depending on citations from the Old Testament, and here—and here only, I believe, in the Acts—do we find an instance of these two closely-related characteristics of the Pauline manner of quotation. The Apostle is represented as quoting together a passage from Isaiah (lv. 3) and a passage from the Psalms (xvi. 10), and as so altering the language of the passage of Isaiah that the words of the prophet have a twofold verbal relation to the words of the Psalter—δώσω ὑμῖν τὰ ὅσια Δαυεὶδ τὰ πιστά[1] . . . οὐ δώσεις τὸν ὅσιόν σου ἰδεῖν διαφθοράν. The point may seem to some a trivial one; but it is trivial mannerisms which are the surest sign of the identity of a writer or a speaker.

The speech in one respect resembles that of St. Stephen, with which it is commonly compared. It opens with a review of the ancient history of Israel. But here all similarity between the two speeches ends. The range and the motive of the reference to the past in the

---

[1] The LXX. runs thus: διαθήσομαι ὑμῖν διαθήκην αἰώνιον, τὰ ὅσια Δαυεὶδ τὰ πιστά. The omission of διαθήκην αἰώνιον, it will be further noted, makes the substitution of δώσω for διαθήσομαι natural.

two utterances are wholly different. St. Stephen was mainly concerned to insist that the earliest crises of revelation were connected with places outside the sacred soil of the Holy Land, and to shew that the rejection of Jesus the Messiah and of His witnesses had its prototype in Israel's rejection of Moses, the divinely-appointed deliverer and law-giver. St. Paul traces the outline of the history in order to prove that in earlier deliverances, as now in the redemption wrought by Jesus the Messiah, all was the direct outcome of the divine working. With David, the kingly type of the Messiah, the review of the past significantly breaks off.

For our present purpose it must suffice to select for consideration three of the characteristic points in the teaching of the sermon.

(1) *The Passion and the Resurrection*. The rejection of Jesus by the rulers of Israel is insisted on here, as in the discourses of St. Peter, which we reviewed in the last lecture. It could not but be a commonplace of the Christian evangelist. Here too, as there, we find an allusion to that passage in Deuteronomy (xxi. 23) which to a Jew invested the cross with the

horrors of the divine curse. But the manner of the reference is not the same in the two speeches. The words in the Pauline sermon are: "When they [*i.e.* those who had asked Pilate that he should be slain] had fulfilled all things that were written of him, they took him down from the tree, and laid him in a tomb" (*v.* 29). The burial (comp. 1 Cor. xv. 4), as well as the "hanging on the tree," is here included in the scope of the allusion. And further, it is the enemies of the Lord who are here said to have laid Him in the tomb[1]—a statement clearly at variance with the history as given alike by the Synoptists and by St. John. Had this version of the story of the Saviour's burial met us in a speech of St. Peter, it could not but have cast a serious suspicion on the fidelity of the record. St. Peter must have known all the history of the day of the Passion far too well to be tempted

---

[1] It is grammatically *possible* to suppose that the subject of καθελόντες . . . ἔθηκαν is indefinite ("men took him down . . . and laid him in a tomb"). But (1) this construction appears to be exceedingly harsh when the series of participles and indicatives (*vv.* 27 f.), all referring to the enemies of the Lord, is observed; (2) the following words ὁ δὲ θεὸς ἤγειρεν κ.τ.λ. seem intended to introduce and emphasize the contrast between the action of God and the action of the Jewish rulers (comp. *e.g.* ii. 23 f., iii. 15).

to manipulate any part of it so as to bring it into conformity with a passage of the Old Testament. The case is otherwise with St. Paul. Doubtless he was familiar with the main outline of the events of the Passion; but it is by no means inconceivable that he was ignorant of the details of the burial of the Lord. St. Luke in the Gospel tells us explicitly of the part in the burial taken by Joseph of Arimathæa; and it seems, therefore, probable that, when here he incorporates in his other Book a different account, we have a sign that he is following closely the report of St. Paul's actual words.

The central fact of the Resurrection is insisted on here, as in St. Peter's discourses. Both speakers are represented as regarding it as the reversal, through God's act, of Israel's rejection. Both speakers are represented as citing what must have been a *locus classicus* with the heralds of the risen Christ—the sixteenth Psalm. But there are clear differences between the Petrine and the Pauline witness. St. Paul here allows to those who were Apostles before him an office in which he could not himself share. They were the primary witnesses of the Resurrection; for they, unlike St. Paul, held converse with the risen Lord among the familiar scenes of earth. Doubtless St. Paul himself believed—nay, he knew—that he had seen the Lord; but his sight of the risen Saviour was different from the sight of Him vouchsafed to the older Apostles. To have explained the nature of his own testimony would have been to draw off the minds of his hearers to a personal history; he therefore rests the authentication of his Gospel of the Resurrection on the witness of the original companions of our Lord. When this is borne in mind, our present passage is seen to be in close harmony with the evidence of the Resurrection as given in 1 Corinthians xv. Again, the aspect of the Resurrection on which St. Paul is represented as dwelling here differs from that which is prominent in the Petrine speeches. Through the Resurrection the Holy One was rescued from a lasting experience of the grave. He should "no longer return into corruption" —to the dishonour and nothingness of the tomb. He had had part in it. He should now have part in it no more. Though the language is wholly different, the thought is precisely that of the Epistle to the Romans (vi. 9): "Christ being raised from the dead dieth no more; death no more hath dominion over him." St. Peter dwelt on the majesty of the risen Jesus. St. Paul emphasizes the thought of His life — His life, which *cannot* henceforth know death.

(2) The consideration of the next point in the speech—its witness to the Lord's Person—in part, at any rate, explains St. Paul's position as to the Resurrection. As long before at Damascus, so here, the Apostle insists on the divine Sonship. But, we ask, in what exact connexion? The passage runs thus: "We bring you good tidings of the promise made unto the fathers, how that God hath fulfilled the same [unto us and[1]] unto our children, in

---

[1] So I venture to restore the text. The reading (ταύτην ὁ θεὸς ἐκπεπλήρωκεν τοῖς τέκνοις ἡμῶν), "which alone has any adequate authority" (Westcott and Hort, *Introduction, Notes on Select Readings*, p. 95), cannot possibly represent what St. Luke intended to write. The simplest solution of the difficulty seems to me to suppose that here, as elsewhere in the Acts (see pp. 81 ff., 284), something has dropped out, and to read ἐκπεπλήρωκεν [ἡμῖν καὶ] τοῖς τέκνοις ἡμῶν. Compare especially ii. 39 (ὑμῖν γάρ ἐστιν ἡ ἐπαγγελία καὶ τοῖς τέκνοις ὑμῶν), Pss. Sol. viii. 39 (ἡμῖν καὶ τοῖς τέκνοις ἡμῶν ἡ εὐδοκία εἰς τὸν αἰῶνα); see also Matt. xxvii. 25, Luke xix. 44, xxiii. 28. The phrase belongs to a type

that he raised up Jesus; as in the second Psalm also it is written, Thou art my Son, this day have I begotten thee. And as concerning that he raised him up from the dead ... he hath spoken on this wise, I will give you the holy mercies of David, which are sure" (*vv.* 32 ff.). Here there are two "raisings up" spoken of, both of which are connected with prophecy. The latter is the raising up from the dead; the former is the raising up to activity, the bringing into the sphere of the world's history.[1] With the former is connected "the promise to David," already referred to in the speech (*v.* 23), "I will *raise up* thy seed after thee" (2 Sam. vii. 12). And in relation to it are the words of the Psalm fulfilled, "This day have I begotten thee," words the primary and historical application of which was to the day when the theocratic king was

common in the Old Testament, *e.g.* Gen. xxxi. 16, Deut. v. 29, xxix. 29.

[1] "The promise made unto the fathers" (*v.* 32) refers rather to the sending of the Messiah than to the Resurrection. Moreover, this allusion to "the promise" connects *v.* 32 with *v.* 23, which deals with the Saviour's entrance upon His ministry. For this sense of ἀναστῆσαι compare iii. 22, 26, vii. 37; v. 30 (ἤγειρεν); and in the LXX. *e.g.* 1 Sam. ii. 35, 2 Sam. xii. 21, Jer. xxiii. 4. The addition of ἐκ νεκρῶν (*v.* 34) differentiates the simple ἀναστήσας of *v.* 32 from the ἀνέστησεν of *v.* 34; compare *vv.* 22, 30.

anointed, when he entered into a new relation to Jehovah, a relation of affiance and obedience on the one side, of fatherly care and guidance on the other. To this "to-day" of the king's anointing, the analogue in the earthly history of the Lord Jesus was the hour when He was endowed with the Father's Spirit, and greeted by the Father's voice, "Thou art my Son."[1] At the Baptism, before the eyes of Israel, and for the work of the ministry, God "raised up Jesus." It was His birthday into the new life of Messianic service and of Messianic Sonship. Death seemed to enter in and destroy this relationship to the Heavenly Father. It was not so. Death was with the Lord Jesus only a brief parenthesis. By the Resurrection it was proved that the covenant with David and his seed was sure and abiding ($\tau\grave{a}$ ὅσια Δαυεὶδ $\tau\grave{a}$ πιστά, $v.$ 34); and that this relation between the living Father and the living Son had not been, and could not be, broken by death. Thus this passage of the Pauline sermon is not at variance

[1] As early as the time of Justin (*Dial.* 88, 103) the words of the voice from Heaven were assimilated to the words of the Psalm; compare Westcott and Hort, *Introduction, Notes on Select Readings*, p. 57; Resch, *Ausscrcanonische Paralleltexte . . . zu Lucas*, pp. 20 ff.

with the Apostle's words to the Roman Church (i. 3 f.)—"Who was born of the seed of David according to the flesh, who was declared to be the Son of God with power, according to the spirit of holiness, by the resurrection of the dead." The teaching of the former passage is presupposed in the latter. In the sermon the Sonship, which was demonstrated anew by the Resurrection, is carried backwards so as to include the whole of the active ministry of the Redeemer.

In this discourse in the synagogue then we listen to St. Paul asserting one aspect of that divine Sonship of Jesus Christ with the proclamation of which he had, in the synagogues of Damascus, begun his ministry. He insists on what we may venture to call an official Sonship, a Sonship, that is, revealed under the earthly conditions of the Lord's ministry. The resurrection to a deathless life, the Apostle teaches, manifested this Sonship as an abiding fact in the eternity to come. From the Epistles it is clear that St. Paul drew from the premises which he here asserts the conclusion which is the faith of the Catholic Church. The

Sonship which did not end with the earthly ministry did not begin with the earthly ministry. The Sonship manifested in the visible order revealed a relation to God which, acknowledging to the full the inadequacy of human language, we call an essential Sonship. "When the fulness of the time came, God sent forth his Son" (Gal. iv. 4). He whom God did not spare for man's sake was "his own Son" (Rom. viii. 32). The Sonship is eternal and unique.[1]

(3) Lastly, St. Paul draws out for his hearers the issue of Christ's redemptive work on earth —"By him every one that believeth is justified from all things, from which ye could not be justified in the law of Moses" (*v.* 39). He offers them in Christ the solution of the great problem which had often perplexed the devout Jew.

It is impossible to read the Epistle to the Romans (especially the seventh and eighth

---

[1] In relation to the "theology" of the Pauline sermon, the passages in the Pauline Epistles which speak of "the Son" are full of instruction —1 Thess. i. 10, 1 Cor. i. 9, xv. 28, 2 Cor. i. 19, Gal. i. 16, ii. 20, iv. 4, 6, Rom. i. 3 (ὃ προεπηγγείλατο . . . περὶ τοῦ υἱοῦ αὐτοῦ), 9, v. 10, viii. 3, 29, 32, Eph. iv. 13, Col. i. 13.

chapters) without being convinced that in the Pharisaic period of his life the Apostle had himself dwelt in the shadow of those awful questionings and uncertainties — How shall sinful man be at peace with God? How can he look for a sentence of acquittal from a just and all-seeing Judge? To some the hope of justification through obedience to the law did not seem impossible. Thus in the *Apocalypse of Baruch* (li. 3) God is represented as speaking of "the glory of those who have now been justified in my law"—"justified in the law," it is, we notice, precisely the phrase which St. Paul here uses ($\dot{\epsilon}\nu$ $\nu\acute{o}\mu\wp$ $\mathrm{M}\omega\nu\sigma\acute{\epsilon}\omega\varsigma$ $\delta\iota\kappa\alpha\iota\omega\theta\hat{\eta}\nu\alpha\iota$). On the other hand, the author of the *Second Book of Esdras* shews that anxious and wistful misgivings forced themselves into the heart of Israelites who realized the sinfulness and the spiritual impotence of man—"For if thou hast a desire to have mercy upon us, then shalt thou be called merciful, to us, namely, that have no works of righteousness. For the just, which have many good works laid up with thee, shall for their own deeds receive reward. . . . In this, O Lord, thy righteousness and thy goodness shall be declared, if thou be merciful unto them which have no store of good works" (viii. 32 ff.). Nay, in that same remarkable book we have a distinct foreshadowing of that conception of faith, as the means whereby man on his part puts himself in contact with the divine compassion, which is so familiar to us in the teaching of St. Paul: "Every one that shall be saved, and shall be able to escape by his works, or by faith, whereby he hath believed . . . shall see my salvation in my land" (ix. 7). Of this supreme problem then St. Paul offers to his fellow-Israelites at Antioch a solution, at once authoritative and historical, in the Messiah, the Son of God, who died and was raised by God from death, "who . . . was raised for our justification" (Rom. iv. 25).

For our present purpose three further points in regard to St. Paul's teaching here claim attention :—(1) There is, as has already appeared, evidence enough to shew that a religious Jew would not be unfamiliar with the vital subject here dealt with, and that the terms which St. Paul here uses would be intelligible to him. (2) It would not be easy to find other words in which St. Paul's doctrine of justification could be so briefly and so forcibly stated. To each phrase and to each turn of a phrase a real parallel can be found in the Epistles of St. Paul, and yet I venture to say that the freedom and naturalness of their combination at once refutes the suggestion that we have here a mosaic of Pauline expressions put together even by a skilful and sympathetic student of the Apostle's writings. (3) And there is another point lurking in the background. In the immediate sequel St. Paul warns his hearers, "lest that come upon you which is spoken in the prophets" (*v.* 40). The reference, it will be observed, is general; but out of the prophetic literature one passage—a passage from Habakkuk (i. 5)—is chosen as a specimen. Why this special choice? Why out of all possible passages is this selected? Is it not because his words in the immediately preceding context—"every one that believeth is justified"—had led St. Paul to quote in the actual speech, or at least had recalled to his mind, that one of his two great proof texts from the Old Testament on the subject of justification which comes from

Habakkuk (ii. 4)—"The just shall live by faith" (Rom. i. 17, Gal. iii. 11)? The same prophet who, as interpreted by St. Paul, tells of the vital energy of faith, is called upon here to pronounce the condemnation of unbelief. If you agree with me in this explanation of the choice of this particular prophetic warning, you will allow that we have a trace of Pauline thought so delicate and so unobtrusive that it can only point to the conclusion that here we have a very close report of St. Paul's words.

2. We turn in the second place to St. Paul's witness to the pagan world.

In his long career as "the Apostle of the nations" St. Paul must often have addressed heathen audiences. Of such speeches two specimens are given in the Acts. The choice of the speech at Athens—addressed to "Greeks," to "the wise" (Rom. i. 14)—needs no comment. But why was the speech at Lystra, so special in its circumstances and aims, chosen as illustrative of his mode of appeal to average men from the pagan world? Its selection, I venture to think, confirms the opinion that St.

Luke's authority for the Pauline speeches was St. Paul himself. Among the many strange episodes in that great missionary life, the events at Lystra were not the least startling. It appealed to St. Paul's grave sense of humour, that he of all men in the world should have been mistaken for one of the gods, and have scarcely been able to restrain his would-be devotees from offering sacrifice to him. Here was indeed a travesty of his own words, "All things to all men." The scene and the words which he then spoke stood out in his memory clear and sharply defined.

(i.) The speech at Lystra (xiv. 15-17) is brief and simple. It has but one main thought —the witness of nature to "the living God."

In one of his Epistles St. Paul reminds the converts from paganism to whom he is writing how, "when [they] were Gentiles, [they] were led away unto those dumb idols, howsoever [they] might be led" (1 Cor. xii. 2). At Lystra he had, as its unwilling victim, to deal with one of those whimsical gusts of superstition to which he seems to refer in his letter. He endeavoured to lay the storm of enthusiasm by assuring the people that he and his companion were "men of like nature" to them, and brought to them "good news," calling on them to "turn from these vain things unto the living God." The language of the Pauline speech, it will be noticed, is singularly parallel to the words with which St. Paul describes the beginning of his work at Thessalonica: "What manner of entering in we had unto you, and how ye turned unto God from idols, to serve a living and true God" (1 Thess. i. 9). The description in the Acts of St. Paul's primary appeal to Gentiles and that in the Epistle are in complete accord. "The living God," to whom St. Paul invites his hearers to turn, is the Creator of "the heaven and the earth and the sea, and all that in them is" (v. 15). It is true that "in the generations gone by" (ἐν ταῖς παρῳχημέναις γενεαῖς; comp. Eph. iii. 5, ἑτέραις γενεαῖς) it seemed that God had left "all the nations" to think and act as they would. Yet, even in those "æonian periods" of silence (Rom. xvi. 25), "he left not himself without witness, in that he did good, and gave you from heaven rains and fruitful seasons, filling your hearts with food and gladness" (*v.* 17).

There is nothing more remarkable, from a literary point of view, about St. Paul's Epistles than the absence from them of any sign that he appreciated the beauties of the world. Metaphors drawn from the stadium, the camp, the world of civic life, are frequent in his writings, and often elaborate. But we find in his Epistles no parables of nature which imply a sympathetic insight into the wonders of the visible order. The scenery through which the traveller passed has left no trace in his writings. The thoughts of God and of man which filled his mind allowed little place for reflexion on the world without.[1] When, however, we read the speech at Lystra, our first impression is that the words here put into St. Paul's mouth are unlike the utterances of the real St. Paul. They seem to be the joyous outpouring of the mind of one who found a solace and an inspiration in the poetry of nature. But when we look beneath the surface, we become conscious that we are

[1] Comp. Jowett, *The Epistles of St. Paul*, ii. p. 455.

mistaken. For in the first place, the words are not a free and spontaneous tribute to the beauty of God's world. They are echoes of the Psalms of Creation. Almost every word is derived from the Old Testament. There appeals to us here, as in the Epistles of St. Paul, not a poet-interpreter of nature, but a student of the Scriptures, who could bring out of that treasury thoughts and words to meet the sudden call. And in the second place, it is the prophet and not the literary artist who speaks. The main thought is not the splendour or the loveliness of the natural world, but the impartial beneficence of God (comp. Matt. v. 45), the simple idea of the ancient Jewish Grace: "Blessed art Thou, Jehovah our God, king of the world, who causest bread to come forth from the earth."[1] "I have always benefited you," God is represented in the *Apocalypse of Baruch* (xiii. 12) as saying to the "peoples and nations," "and you have always denied the beneficence."

It is important for our purpose to compare the teaching here put into St. Paul's mouth

[1] Edersheim, *Life and Times of Jesus the Messiah*, i. p. 684.

with the teaching on the same subject found in his Epistles.

(*a*) There are two views of nature, both of which appeal to us according to our varying moods. We exult in its beauty and its graciousness. We are saddened by its strange and awful tragedies. These two views are not mutually exclusive; they are rather complementary. Both find expression in St. Paul's writings. On the one hand, he looks out on "the creation subjected to vanity." "The whole creation groaneth and travaileth in pain together until now." It is true that the sorrow which we trace everywhere is no hopeless, purposeless misery; it is the pangs of birth which shall issue in a fuller and a higher life, the pledge of a complete redemption. But "the deliverance from the bondage of corruption" and the entrance "into the liberty of the glory of the children of God" are not yet (Rom. viii. 19 ff.).[1] On the other hand, though, as we have already seen, the Apostle never dwells on the beauty of the world, and though he characteristically and habitually lives among thoughts suggested by

[1] Comp. Bishop Westcott, *The Gospel of Life*, pp. 240 ff.

God's grace in redemption rather than by His bounty in creation, yet he enforces the lesson that "God giveth us richly all things to enjoy" (1 Tim. vi. 17). Hence, at least in part, springs his abiding spirit of thankfulness and contentment (*e.g.* 1 Thess. v. 17, Phil. iv. 4 ff., 10-20). To the healthy mind of St. Paul God's creation is a good and happy world. The Apostle makes the words of the Psalm his own: "The earth is the Lord's, and the fulness thereof" (1 Cor. x. 26). "God created [meats] to be received with thanksgiving by them that believe and know the truth. For every creature of God is good, and nothing is to be rejected, if it be received with thanksgiving" (1 Tim. iv. 3 f.). The words of the Pauline speech, echoing the fervour of the Psalter, are the vivid presentation of thoughts which find an occasional and more restrained expression among the arguments and exhortations of the Epistles.

(*b*) St. Paul is represented in the Acts as leading his hearers at Lystra upwards through nature to God. The lavish bounty of nature is a "witness" to the goodness of the Creator, and constitutes a claim on His part to man's undivided allegiance. The one passage in St. Paul's Epistles in which he deals at length with the state of the heathen world supplies a close parallel to his alleged utterance here. "The invisible things of him since the creation of the world are clearly seen, being perceived through the things that are made, even his everlasting power and divinity; that they may be without excuse: because that, knowing God, they glorified him not as God, neither gave thanks; but became vain in their reasonings, and their senseless heart was darkened . . . [They] changed the glory of the incorruptible God for the likeness of an image of corruptible man, and of birds, and four-footed beasts, and creeping things" (Rom. i. 20 ff.). In both passages, it will be observed, the visible world is regarded as a revelation of God. In the Epistle, indeed, it is viewed rather as a manifestation of His awful power; in the speech rather as a manifestation of His generous goodness; but the words, "neither gave thanks," in the former shew that the idea of the divine beneficence, emphasized in the speech, is not wholly absent from the words of the Epistle. In both passages men's blindness towards the witness of nature is connected with their degraded conception of the Divine; they worshipped "vain things," and so, becoming assimilated to the objects of their worship, they themselves "became vain" (comp. Eph. iv. 17).

One further point in regard to the speech at Lystra calls for remark. There is not a single word in it from beginning to end which stamps it as Christian. The reference, indeed, to God's apparent abandonment of "all the nations" "*in the generations gone by*" implies on the speaker's part a belief that a new epoch had now begun. But nothing is said as to what is the dividing line between the past and the present. There is no hint of the work of Jesus Christ or of His expected return (contrast 1 Thess. i. 9 f.). The words which the historian here puts into the mouth of St. Paul might be, in fact, the words of any pious Jew who regarded himself as commissioned by God to make proselytes from idolatry. The circumstances, it is true, when we consider them, amply explain this remarkable reticence. The speaker's aim for the moment was not to evangelize, but to prevent an act of idolatry. Moreover the narrative plainly implies that the scene was full of confusion—"scarce restrained they the multitude"; doubtless the speech was often interrupted and perhaps ended abruptly. But a study of the apocryphal Acts shews us that no romancer would have been so self-restrained and courageous as to invent a Pauline speech destitute of any reference to Christ and Christ's work (see *e.g. Acta Pauli et Theclae*, 17). The silence of St. Paul's speech at Lystra as to these essential topics is a very strong proof of its truthfulness.

(ii.) The right understanding of St. Paul's speech at Athens (xvii. 22-31) depends largely on the interpretation of the circumstances which led up to it, and of the occasion of its delivery (xvii. 16-21).

The centre of the busy life of Athens was the Agora. Here day after day St. Paul was to be found reasoning with any who "happened to be there." Among these, the historian tells us parenthetically, were "some of the Epicurean and Stoic philosophers." Opinion generally about him was divided. Some were content to wonder what could be the meaning of "this glib adventurer's" words (τί ἂν θέλοι ὁ σπερμολόγος[1] οὗτος λέγειν). Others started the half-mocking theory that he was a *Socrates redivivus*,[2] introducing strange or foreign deities, a new god of healing, Ἰησοῦς, and a new companion goddess, Ἀνάστασις.[3]

---

[1] "Sine dubio hoc ex ipso ore Atheniensium auctor excepit" (Blass *in loco*). If for "auctor" we substitute "S. Paulus," the words are probably true. St. Paul was struck with the slang term by which the Athenians described him (comp. τῶν ὑπερλίαν ἀποστόλων, 2 Cor. xi. 5, xii. 11), and St. Luke learned it from him. The word σπερμολόγος is used of an adventurer who picks up a "hand to mouth" living; comp. *e.g.* Dem. *de Cor.* 269. 19, σπερμολόγος, περίτριμμα ἀγορᾶς : Philo *Leg. ad Caium* 30 (ii. 576, ed. Mangey), Ἑλίκωνι τῷ εὐπατρίδῃ, δούλῳ σπερμολόγῳ, περιτρίμματι, καὶ Ἀπελλῇ τινι τραγῳδῷ, ὃς ... ἐκαπήλευσε τὴν ὥραν, ἔξωρος δὲ γενόμενος ἐπὶ τὴν σκηνὴν παρῆλθεν. The language of such persons was, and is, plentiful and (on occasion) low; comp. Plutarch ii. 664 A, ταῦτα μὲν περίεργα καὶ σπερμολογικά : id. ii. 456 C, ἀκόλαστα καὶ πικρὰ καὶ σπερμολογικὰ ῥήματα. Hence the following definitions : *Etym. Magnum*, ὁ εὐτελὴς καὶ εὐκαταφρόνητος ἄνθρωπος καὶ ἴσως ἀπὸ τῶν ἀλλοτρίων διαζῶν : *Hesych.*, φλύαρος : *Suidas*, εὐρύλογος ἀκριτόμυθος : *Onom. Vetus*, λάλος. For such Jewish adventurers compare xix. 13 (τῶν περιερχομένων Ἰουδαίων ἐξορκιστῶν) and the description of Simon (viii. 9 ff.) and of Elymas (xiii. 6 ff.).

[2] Compare Xen. *Memor.* i. 1, ἀδικεῖ Σωκράτης ... καινὰ δαιμόνια εἰσφέρων : Plato *Apol.* xii. (24 B), Σωκράτη φησὶν ἀδικεῖν ... θεοὺς οὓς ἡ πόλις νομίζει οὐ νομίζοντα ἕτερα δὲ δαιμόνια καινά.

[3] The name Ἰησοῦς, otherwise unintelligible, would be naturally connected by the Athenians with ἴασις (Ionic ἴησις) and Ἰασώ (Ἰησώ),

At length a crisis came. The frequent dialogues in the Agora led up to the long address which formed an epoch in St. Paul's missionary life. Who asked for this exposition of St. Paul's teaching? Where was it delivered, and before whom? It is impossible here fully to discuss the various answers which have been given to these questions. It must suffice briefly to say that there appears to me to be nothing in the narrative or in the speech itself to support,

---

the goddess of healing and health (*e.g.* Ar. *Plut.* 701). We may compare the *paronomasia* in Acts ix. 34, ἰᾶταί σε Ἰησοῦς Χριστός. For Ἀνάστασις compare ἀναστατήρια (Hesych.) in the sense of sacrifices offered on recovery from sickness. The personification would hardly seem strange to men accustomed to the personification of Ὑγίεια (see Frazer, *Pausanias*, ii. pp. 277 ff.). This interpretation of the words Ἰησοῦς and ἀνάστασις would be confirmed in the minds of the Athenians, if they caught the words σωτηρία and σωτήρ in St. Paul's teaching. The latter was a title of Asclepios (*e.g. C.I.G.* 1222, 1755; comp. Thraemer in Pauly-Wissowa, *Real-Encycl.* II. ii. 1677. 47 ff.), and the term σωτήρια denoted sacrifices for recovery (Herod. i. 10).

I am indebted to Mr. A. B. Cook for the following remarks: "The Ionic form Ἰησώ was doubtless known at Athens from such passages as Herondas iv. 6 (cult of Ἰησώ in Kos):

Πανάκη τε κἠπιώ τε κἰησὼ χαίροι.

It might be worth while considering whether there was any confusion with a deity far better known than Ἰασώ, I mean Isis. She too was a health goddess; in fact her name was later derived from Hebr. *iasa* = 'salvavit' (Roscher, *Lex. d. Mythologie*, II. i. 522. 42). She bore the title σώτειρα (*ibid.* 46), and was credited with the discovery of the drug ἀθανασία (Diod. i. 25)."

much indeed to refute, the theory that St. Paul stood before the Court of the Areopagus in the *Stoa Basileios*, whether (*a*) as one arraigned for a preliminary investigation before a religious tribunal, or (*b*) as one brought by the philosophers before the authorities of the city, that so the exposition of his doctrine might receive a higher importance, or again, (*c*) as a teacher appearing before a board entrusted with the regulation of the lectures of the university.[1]

---

[1] (*a*) The view that St. Paul was brought before the Court of the Areopagus has been a favourite one since early days. Thus Chrysostom (Migne, *P. G.* lx. 268) says : ἦγον αὐτὸν ἐπὶ τὸν Ἄρειον Πάγον, οὐχ ὥστε μαθεῖν ἀλλ' ὥστε κολάσαι· ἔνθα αἱ φονικαὶ δίκαι. In recent times this view has been maintained in a somewhat different form, viz. : that St. Luke describes here a "preliminary investigation" (προδικασία), and that ἐπὶ τὸν Ἄρειον Πάγον (*v.* 19, comp. *v.* 22) is equivalent to ἐπὶ τὴν βουλὴν τὴν ἐξ Ἀρείου Πάγου or ἐπὶ τὴν ἐν Ἀρείῳ Πάγῳ βουλήν. So E. Curtius (*Die Stadtgeschichte von Athen*, 1891, pp. 262 f.) : The Apostle "was led by those whom he had most bitterly irritated to the King's Hall, where those cases which were to be decided by the Areopagus were taken. . . . Here it had first to be determined whether a charge of introducing new deities was established ; and here the Apostle was able, in front of the King's Hall, in the midst of the representatives of the Areopagus, in the hearing of a great concourse of people, to make the speech in which he refuted the charge." (*b*) Curtius, however, soon modified his interpretation of the incident, and in his *Paulus in Athen* (printed in his *Gesammelte Abhandlungen*, 1894, ii. pp. 527 ff.) he put forward another theory : "The report of a διδαχὴ καινή of quite a peculiar kind spread ; the market-place was filled with an expectant crowd of native Athenians and strangers, and the philosophers, who were here the spokesmen, were impelled to measure swords with the

The historian himself explains the circumstances of the speech with sufficient clearness. The courteous request which called forth this speech he puts into the mouth, not of any official persons, but of those whom in the Agora the Apostle had already interested. He explains the motive and the spirit of the request by a reference to the passion for "telling or hearing some new thing" which characterized all the inhabitants of Athens. As the sequel of the speech, he records not a judicial decision, however informal, but a division of opinion. Some, as St. Paul broke off, "were mocking"; others expressed a hope that they might again hear the speaker discuss these matters. The speech itself confirms what appears to be the natural interpretation of the narrative. It is addressed not to Areopagites (whether regarded as magistrates or as university officials), but generally to an Athenian audience ($ἄνδρες$ $Ἀθηναῖοι$, $v.$ 22); and it has nothing in it which suggests that it

teacher who had thus presented himself. In order to satisfy their curiosity, they invite a fuller statement on Paul's part, and endeavour to lend a higher significance to the expected speech by getting the magistrates of the city to take part in the matter ($ἤγαγον$ $ἐπὶ$ $τὸν$ $Ἄρειον$ $πάγον$)" (p. 528). (*c*) The third view mentioned in the text above is that of Professor Ramsay (*St. Paul the Traveller*, pp. 243 ff.).

is an *apologia*. The story of the speech, then, as I read St. Luke's narrative, was simple and natural. St. Paul for many days had discoursed with Athenians and with "strangers sojourning there," as they came and went, amid the bustle and concourse of the Agora. One day some of those who had heard fragments of his teaching, feeling a keener curiosity than the rest as to his real meaning, wished to give him a quieter hearing. "Taking hold of him" (comp. ix. 27, xxiii. 19), that they might give kindly guidance and help to one who was a stranger and perhaps physically weak, they led him up the steep stone steps which ascended from the Agora to the Areopagus. On the way they asked him to repeat to them in a more connected form what he had often said in the Agora below. The area of the summit is small. They made, therefore, a circle round the Apostle, some taking their place on the stone seats which still surround the hill[1]; and the speaker himself,

[1] "A flight of fifteen or sixteen steps cut in the rock, but now ruinous, leads up from the south-eastern side of the hill to a small artificially levelled platform on the top of the hill, where there are some remains of rock-hewn seats" (Frazer, *Pausanias's Description of Greece*, ii. pp. 362 f.).

naturally enough, "stood in the midst of the Areopagus."

Let us consider St. Paul's treatment in the speech at Athens of three topics—the heathen world and its idolatry, the doctrine of God, the divine call to repentance.

(*a*) The Heathen World and its Idolatry.

In his Epistles St. Paul is silent as to the æsthetic aspect of pagan worship. Of its sense of awe, its solemnity, its stateliness, its poetic interpretation of nature, its influence as a means of artistic culture, its close relation to literatures unsurpassed in strength and grace—of all this St. Paul, as he reveals himself to us in his letters, is absolutely unconscious. To his mind, full of the sense of God's presence and power, all this is as though it were not. At least for the worship of the elements—"fire, or wind, or swift air, or circling stars, or raging water, or luminaries of heaven"—the writer of the Book of Wisdom finds excuse. "If it was through delight in their beauty that they took them to be gods . . . for these men there is but small blame; for they too peradventure do but go astray while they are seeking God and desiring to find him" (Wisd. xiii. 2-6). But the Apostle of the Gentiles in his letters speaks of Gentile idolatry as a system wholly degraded and wholly degrading. They "changed the glory of the incorruptible God for the likeness of an image of corruptible man, and of birds, and four-footed beasts, and creeping things. . . . They exchanged the truth of God for a lie, and worshipped and served the creature rather than the Creator" (Rom. i. 23 ff.). At Athens, if anywhere in the world, some relaxation of this stern unbending attitude might have been pardoned. At least a Gentile historian, if he were drawing on his own imagination, would have let slip, we should suppose, some expression of appreciation for the glories of Athenian art. But it is not so. Neither in the narrative nor in the speech is there a single word which is at variance with what we know to have been St. Paul's view of idolatry. As he wandered about the city and "scrutinized the objects of [its] worship" (xvii. 23), he was always and everywhere moved to a deep sense of exasperation. "His spirit was provoked ($παρωξύνετο$) within him, as he beheld the city full of idols."

"Have we ever realised the force of that single word, with which the historian describes the impression left on the Apostle's mind by this far-famed city? Gazing on the most sublime and beautiful creations of Greek art, the masterpieces of Pheidias and Praxiteles, he has no eye for their beauty or their sublimity. He pierces through the veil of the material and the transitory; and behind this semblance of grace and glory the true nature of things reveals itself. To him this chief centre of human culture and intelligence, this

> Eye of Greece, mother of arts
> And eloquence,

appears only as κατείδωλος, overrun with idols, beset with phantoms which mislead, and vanities which corrupt."[1] The speech itself is in complete harmony with the narrative. Its opening words, though they are often interpreted as expressive of commendation, are in reality words of rebuke not wholly unmingled with contempt—"In all things I perceive that ye are very superstitious" (ὡς δεισιδαιμονεστέρους[2]). In

[1] Bishop Lightfoot, *Cambridge Sermons*, pp. 302 f.

[2] Theophrastus draws a contemptuous picture of the δεισιδαίμων, and defines δεισιδαιμονία as δειλία πρὸς τὸ δαιμόνιον. Menander wrote

no other sense could the word be understood by Athenians, who would instinctively recall the literary associations of the word, still less by the philosophers among St. Paul's audience, who themselves despised and ridiculed the popular religion, to which, nevertheless, from motives of convenience they conformed.

On two grounds St. Paul is here represented as condemning idolatry. In the first place the shrines, local habitations of deities, and the material cults connected with them, were in

a comedy called δεισιδαίμων. In Aristotle *Politics* v. 11 δεισιδαιμονία is regarded as commonly open to the charge of "stupidity" (ἀβελτερία). Comp. Polyb. vi. 56, δοκεῖ τὸ παρὰ τοῖς ἄλλοις ἀνθρώποις ὀνειδιζόμενον, τοῦτο συνέχειν τὰ Ῥωμαίων πράγματα, λέγω δὲ τὴν δεισιδαιμονίαν. See Jebb's *Theophrastus*, pp. 263 f., Wetstein *ad locum*, and Field, *Notes on Translation of the New Testament*, pp. 125 f. In point of fact, the words ὡς δεισιδαιμονεστέρους give, in a form as little offensive as possible, St. Paul's view of Athenian idolatry already noticed by the historian (*v.* 16)—παρωξύνετο τὸ πνεῦμα αὐτοῦ ἐν αὐτῷ θεωροῦντος κατείδωλον οὖσαν τὴν πόλιν. Field, however, thinks that the comparative serves to soften the censure—"somewhat," "rather"—quoting Diog. Laert. ii. 132, ἦν δέ πως καὶ ἠρέμα καὶ δεισιδαιμονέστερος, and Hor. *Sat.* i. 9. 71, "sum paulo infirmior"; but in the former of these passages the ἠρέμα and in the latter the *paulo* indicate the slightness of the quality referred to, and give a special tone to the comparative. For the quasi-superlative force of the comparative, compare *v.* 21, ἢ λέγειν τι ἢ ἀκούειν τι καινότερον. On the other hand, the ὡς does appear to have a mitigating force; it brings out the fact that the word δεισιδαιμονεστέρους expresses the speaker's own impression.

flagrant contradiction to the true conception of God as the Creator, and therefore as the Sovereign Lord, of all things. Here, at least in theory, the Stoics were at one with the Christian Apostle. Secondly, it was a commonplace with Greek poets that men are "the offspring of God." That men, therefore, should teach that the Father of men—the Divine Being—"is like unto gold, or silver, or stone, graven by art and device of man," is a self-inflicted insult. The times when such conceptions and practices prevailed could only be regarded as "times of ignorance" (comp. Eph. iv. 18)—ignorance of God, of the true meaning of the world, and of the true dignity of man (comp. Rom. i. 24 ff.). With this verdict of "ignorance" on the Gentile world St. Paul's teaching in the Epistles corresponds. In the Epistle to the Romans (i. 21; comp. *v.* 19), it is true, the Apostle speaks of the heathen as "knowing God" (γνόντες τὸν θεόν). But this "knowledge" appears to mean a recognition of the existence of a divine Power which, through their own fault, did not issue in an apprehension of the true attributes of God and of His claims on man, and which was barren of result in true worship and true thankfulness. "They knew God," but "they refused to have God in their knowledge" (*v.* 28). Elsewhere, however, without qualification, St. Paul speaks, as he is represented in the Acts as speaking at Athens, of the "ignorance" of the nations—"the nations which know not God" (1 Thess. iv. 5, Gal. iv. 8); "the world through its wisdom knew not God" (1 Cor. i. 21); Christian converts must remember the time when they were "without God ($ἄθεοι$) in the world" (Eph. ii. 12).

In the Epistles the Apostle draws a still darker picture of idolatry. It was hopeless in face of death (1 Thess. iv. 13, Eph. ii. 12). In the sphere of social and personal life it bore its natural fruit in a luxuriant harvest of vile licentiousness (1 Thess. iv. 5, Rom. i. 24 ff., Col. iii. 5 ff., Eph. iv. 19). Behind it there lay a mysterious and awful background, the working and the worship of the powers of evil (1 Cor. x. 20). Of these hideous traits in the portraiture of idolatry nothing is said in the Pauline speech at Athens. The omission is natural and true to the realities of a missionary's work. The

Apostle stood before the Athenians as an ambassador. If faithfulness to the sovereign Power which sends him is one supreme characteristic of the ambassador's office, the object of his mission is to conciliate. He must win, before he delivers in the fulness of its severity his message of rebuke.

One ray of light in the blackness of idolatry which surrounded him at Athens the Apostle discerned—"a beam in darkness; let it grow." If he had no eye for the triumphs of Athenian art, the altar "to the unknown God" (ἀγνώστῳ θεῷ) arrested his attention. Doubtless it was in reality the outcome of "superstition" (δεισιδαιμονία). In some visitation of plague or famine it was not obvious what god needed propitiation. Fear suggested an expedient. An altar was erected to the god, whosoever he might be, whose hand was heavy on the people.[1] No name could be assigned to him; the inscription must needs be, "To the unknown God." But to St. Paul those two pathetic words of anxious, scrupulous ignorance seemed to reveal an un-

---

[1] Compare Diog. Laert. i. 10. 110, *Epimen.* θύειν τῷ προσήκοντι θεῷ. On altars to unknown gods see Frazer, *Pausanias*, ii. pp. 33 ff.

conscious recognition of the one Creator and Father of all; they witnessed to a blind "groping" after Him who "is not far from each one of us." He is eager to welcome an act of unconscious worship, just as in the Epistle to the Romans (ii. 14 ff.; comp. ix. 30) he looks forward to that day "when God shall judge the secrets of men" as a revelation of lives ennobled by unconscious obedience to the divine law.

This discussion of St. Paul's view as to the attitude of "the nations" towards God naturally leads on to the consideration of the Apostle's teaching in regard to God's attitude towards "the nations." St. Paul, as he did his work as Christ's herald among the heathen, must often have been oppressed by anxious questionings as to God's dealings, especially in the ages past, with the world of heathenism, of which the Evangelist could now only touch the fringe. How could he justify to himself and to others the divine ways? St. Paul, of course, never enters on a discussion of the origin of idolatry in its different forms. Such an investigation would have been alien to the age and to his own habits of thought. He touches on the problem incidentally, and under the necessary limitations of his religious training and his own field of observation. In the Epistles we find two antithetical lines of thought. On the one hand there is a view—suggested largely by the sights and tales of heinous sin which must have made up much of his experience in the cities and villages of the Empire—which lays stress on God's retributive justice. The heathen, deaf to God's voice speaking to them in conscience, "gave themselves up (ἑαυτοὺς παρέδωκαν) to lasciviousness, to work all uncleanness with covetousness" (Eph. iv. 19). God set His seal on their habitual action. "God gave them up (παρέδωκεν αὐτούς) in the lusts of their hearts unto uncleanness"; "God gave them up unto passions of dishonour"; "God gave them up unto a reprobate mind" (Rom. i. 24, 26, 28). The pagan world lived under a sentence, on God's side, of judicial abandonment. This conception, explicitly stated in the Epistles, appears, in its simplest form, and divested (as would be natural) of its awful sternness, in the brief address to the people of Lystra—"[God] in the generations gone by suffered all the nations to walk in their own ways" (xiv. 16). But on the other hand there is another view presented in St. Paul's Epistles which magnifies the divine mercy. God, imperilling, as it were, His character as absolutely holy, refrained from visiting the sins of the heathen world with a punishment commensurate with them, till the discipline of judicial abandonment had done its work, and "the fulness of time" came for His secret purpose of universal redemption and renewal to be revealed. The different elements of thought which I have ventured thus to combine in a single statement are found scattered throughout the Epistles—"God hath shut up all unto disobedience, that he might have mercy upon all" (Rom. xi. 32; comp. Gal. iii. 22); "God purposed [Jesus Christ] to be a propitiation, through faith, by his blood, to shew his righteousness, because of the passing over of the sins done afore time (διὰ τὴν πάρεσιν τῶν προγεγονότων ἁμαρτημάτων), in the forbearance (ἐν τῇ ἀνοχῇ) of God; for the shewing, I say, of his righteousness at this present season" (Rom. iii. 25 f.); "The revelation of the mystery which hath been kept in silence through times eternal, but now is manifested, and ... is made known unto all the nations unto obedience of faith" (Rom. xvi. 25 f.); "The mystery of Christ, which in other generations was not made known unto the sons of men, as it hath now been revealed unto his holy apostles and prophets in the Spirit; to wit, that the Gentiles are fellow-heirs, and fellow-members of the body, and fellow-partakers of the promise in Christ through the gospel" (Eph. iii. 4 ff.; comp. Eph. i. 9, iii. 9, Col. i. 25 ff.). Corresponding to this conception of the divine dispensations we have the sentence in the speech at Athens: "The times of ignorance therefore God overlooked (ὑπεριδών); but now he declareth to men that they shall all everywhere repent" (v. 30). The language and the thought of these words are alike eminently Pauline. The phrase "all men everywhere" (πάντας πανταχοῦ) belongs to a type familiar in St. Paul's writings (*e.g.* 1 Cor. iv. 17, 2 Cor. ix. 8, Eph. v. 20, Phil. i. 3). The "but now" (τὰ νῦν) draws the contrast between the past characterized by silence on the divine side and sin on man's side, and on the other hand the present with revelation and redemption on God's part and the possibilities of renewal for man —a contrast to which St. Paul in his writings habitually recurs (*e.g.* Rom. xvi. 26, Gal. iv. 9, Eph. iii. 5, v. 8, Col. i. 26). Further, in the great passage from Romans iii. quoted above St. Paul asserts that the propitiation wrought out by Christ, the final condemnation and removal of sin through the sacrifice of Himself, was designed by God as a decisive vindication of His righteousness, a vindication which was necessary because in His forbearance (ἐν τῇ ἀνοχῇ, not ἐν τῇ χάριτι) He had, without punishment or atonement, passed over (διὰ τὴν πάρεσιν, not διὰ τὴν ἄφεσιν) men's sins in the long epochs of the past. The ideas of God's patience and His apparent indifference to sin, emphasized in the passage of the Epistle, find vivid and exact expression in the statement of the Pauline speech that "The times of ignorance God overlooked."[1]

---

[1] With Acts xvii. 30 (ὑπεριδὼν . . . τοῖς ἀνθρώποις . . . μετανοεῖν) compare Wisd. xi. 23, παρορᾷς ἁμαρτήματα ἀνθρώπων εἰς μετάνοιαν. The coincidence is too close to be accidental. The passage in Rom. i. dealing with the heathen world and the Pauline speeches in Acts xiv., xvii.,

(*b*) The Doctrine of God.

The teaching of the speech which comes under this head, so far as I have not anticipated it in the previous section, may be conveniently considered in relation to (i.) the unity of the race; (ii.) the unity of history; (iii.) the unity of human life.

(i.) *The Doctrine of God and the Unity of the Race.*—God "made the world and all things therein" (*v.* 24). "He made of one (ἐξ ἑνός) every nation of men" (*v.* 26). The speaker had probably two special reasons for asserting

---

alike reflect the thoughts and to some extent the language of the Book of Wisdom. The parallels between Rom. i. and Wisdom are given at length in Sanday and Headlam's *Romans*, pp. 51 f. "While on the one hand," to quote their summing up, "there can be no question of direct quotation, on the other hand the resemblance is so strong both as to the main lines of the argument (i. Natural religion discarded, ii. idolatry, iii. catalogue of immorality) and in the details of thought and to some extent of expression as to make it clear that at some time in his life St. Paul must have bestowed upon the Book of Wisdom a considerable amount of study." Even in the report of the speeches at Lystra and Athens contained in the Acts, condensed and (to some extent) edited as that report must be, parallels with Wisdom of the same kind as those noticed in Rom. i. reveal themselves. See, *e.g.*, Acts xiv. 17 ∥ Wisd. xiii. 1 *b*; Acts xvii. 23, 30 ∥ Wisd. xiv. 22, xv. 11; Acts xvii. 24 ∥ Wisd. xiii. 3 *b*, 4 *b*, 9 *c*; Acts. xvii. 27 ∥ Wisd. xiii. 6 *c*, 9 *c*; Acts xvii. 29 ∥ Wisd. xiii. 10, xv. 4; Acts xvii. 30 ∥ Wisd. xi. 23. The existence of such a common literary characteristic as this confirms the conclusion that the Epistle and the two Pauline speeches are the production of the same mind.

this doctrine. On the one hand, it negatived the traditional boast of the Athenians that, as αὐτόχθονες, they were not as other men. On the other hand, it coincided, so far at least as its language was concerned, with the views of the nobler Stoics of the period—views in which they characteristically diverged from the position of the Epicureans. The qualification in the foregoing statement as to the Stoics will be noted. The coincidence, however telling, could only be momentary and superficial. For the Stoic and the Christian doctrines rested on different foundations. The Stoic based his belief in the unity of the race on his assertion of a common material origin, the Christian teacher on his conviction that all things and all men have their one source in a personal God and Father. This seems to be the meaning of the ἐξ ἑνός ("of one"; comp. Hebr. ii. 11) in this passage. The reference is to the one Creator Himself. This conception of God as the source as well as the maker of the universe is familiar to us in St. Paul's Epistles—"There is one God, the Father, of whom (ἐξ οὗ) are all things" (1 Cor. viii. 6; comp. xi. 12, Rom.

xi. 36, Eph. iv. 6). A close parallel to the words under discussion (notwithstanding difference of expression) is found in Eph. iii. 14, "The Father from whom every family in heaven and earth is named" (ἐξ οὗ πᾶσα πατριὰ ... ὀνομάζεται). In the Epistles, indeed, the Apostle goes a stage further, and traces this thought of the unity of the race onward to its realization. Redemption reaffirms the oneness of the nations. In Christ the ideal becomes a practical reality. "There can be neither Jew nor Greek, there can be neither bond nor free, there can be no male and female; for ye are all one man in Christ Jesus" (Gal. iii. 28; comp. *e.g.* Col. iii. 11, Eph. ii. 15 ff.).

(ii.) *The Doctrine of God and the Unity of History.*—"He made of one every nation of men for to dwell on all the face of the earth, determining their appointed seasons and the bounds of their habitation" (*v.* 26). The history of the world is the evolution of the Creator's first purpose. The periods of that history— the epochs of national progress and decline— are not, as the Stoics taught, the outcome of blind destiny. They subserve the divine will, which is their source and law. So, I think, we may draw out the meaning of the words, "determining their appointed seasons." In the Pauline Epistles we have no precise parallel to them, dealing (at least primarily), as they do, with the history of the nations. But the same conception of divinely ordained periods and seasons is familiar to us in the Epistles in reference to redemption—"When the fulness of the time came, God sent forth his Son" (Gal. iv. 4); "His good pleasure which he purposed in him unto a dispensation of the fulness of the seasons" (Eph. i. 9 f.); "The dispensation of the mystery which from all ages hath been hid in God who created all things" (Eph. iii. 9; comp. 1 Tim. ii. 6, vi. 15, Titus i. 3). The Epistles agree with the speech in sketching the outline of a divine philosophy of history.

(iii.) *The Doctrine of God and the Unity of Human Life.*—" He is not far from each one of us: for in him we live and move and have our being; as certain even of your own poets have said, For we are also his offspring" (*vv.* 27 f.). The fact that the speaker chooses a half verse of a Stoic poet[1] as typical of the recognition in Greek poetry generally of the Fatherhood of God, indicates that he has in his mind Stoic language as to the nearness of God to man. Such language was often noble and devout. "No work on earth is wrought apart from Thee, O God," says Cleanthes (*Hymn to Zeus* 15 f.), "nor in the divine vault of heaven, nor in the sea." "God is near thee; He is with thee; He is within," is a saying of Seneca (*Ep. Mor.* xli. 1). But the language of Stoic devotion is robbed of its beauty and meaning by Stoic dogma. "God" is merely a synonym for "nature." He "is at once universal matter and the creative force which fashions matter into the particular materials out of which things are made.[2]" The Christian preacher, appealing to their conventional language rather than to their formal dogmas, strove to win the Stoics among his audience. He would fain take them with him as far as they could go. But in truth only by a sacrifice of the principles of their philosophy

---

[1] The precise words occur in Aratus *Phenom.* 5; comp. Cleanthes *Hymn to Zeus* 4 (ἐκ σοῦ γὰρ γένος ἐσμέν).

[2] Zeller, *The Stoics, Epicureans, and Sceptics*, Eng. trans., p. 149.

could they share his thoughts of God. For Stoic theology (if the word may be used) was a materialistic pantheism. To the Christian teacher God was a Person; and in regard to the presence of God in creation, Christian theology holds with equal firmness a belief in the immanence of God in the world, and a belief in the transcendence of God above the world. The latter idea, the necessary corrective of the former, is recognized in the Pauline speech through the simple statement that God is the Creator, the Lord of heaven and earth. The doctrine of the divine transcendence finds expression, it need hardly be said, in numberless passages of St. Paul's Epistles. The doctrine of the divine immanence, which is specially characteristic of this speech, and which is here presented in its simplest and most general form, is stated in its strictly theological aspect in that passage of St. Paul's Epistle to the Colossians where he dwells on the Son's mediatorship in the world of nature as well as in the world of grace. He is "the first-born of all creation; for in him were all things created, in the heavens and upon the earth, things visible and things invisible ... all things have been created through him, and *unto him* (εἰς αὐτόν); and he is before all things, and *in him all things consist* (τὰ πάντα ἐν αὐτῷ συνέστηκεν), and he is the head of the body, the church, etc." (Col. i. 15 ff.). Again, in the Epistle to the Ephesians St. Paul, in two memorable phrases, indicates the close relation of the redemptive and the cosmic functions of the Son: "He [*i.e.* the Father] ... gave him to be head over all things to the church, which is his body, the fulness of *him that filleth all in all*" (i. 22 f.). "He ... ascended far above all the heavens, that he might *fill all things*" (iv. 10). These two latter passages in particular present the Apostle's matured conception of the nearness of God to the world—a truth which finds expression in the epigram of the missionary speech, "In him [*i.e.* God] we live and move and have our being."

Such is the doctrine of God contained in the speech. The greatest of Athenian philosophers had once said: " To find out the Father and Maker of all this universe is a hard task. And when we have found Him, to speak of Him to all men is impossible" (Plato, *Timaeus* 28 c). The preacher on the Areopagus, like the Apostle who speaks in the Epistles, claims that he knows the secret — τὸ μυστήριον τῆς εὐσεβείας—and that he is commissioned to proclaim what he knows. "What ye worship (εὐσεβεῖτε) in ignorance, this set I forth to you" (*v.* 23).

(*c*) The Divine Call to Repentance.

In the Stoic doctrine of God as Matter, Force, Destiny, there was no room for a belief either in divine righteousness or in human responsibility. Man lived and acted in the chains of a physical law of constraint. It is true that here as elsewhere the language of Stoic writers rose to a level far above that of their formal tenets. But the dogmas of Stoicism knew nothing of a sense of sin. For the sake of the Stoics especially among his hearers, it was a matter of primary importance that the Christian preacher should affirm that God is "the moral Governor of the world," and that man is responsible to Him. "Now [God] declareth to men that they should all everywhere repent: inasmuch as he hath appointed a day, in the which he will judge the world in righteousness by the man whom he hath ordained; whereof he hath given assurance unto all men, in that he raised him from the dead" (*vv.* 30 f.). The visit to Athens stands midway between St. Paul's evangelization of Thessalonica and his visit to Corinth, where the two Epistles to the Thessalonians were written. These letters shew that at this period of his ministry St. Paul's mind was filled with the expectation of Christ's return as the Judge. "His preaching [at Thessalonica] seems to have turned mainly upon one point—the approaching judgment, the coming of Christ. . . . Around this one doctrine the Apostle's practical warnings and exhortations had clustered.[1]" We have already seen how one element in his proclamation of the Gospel at Thessalonica had a place, as was indeed inevitable, in his appeal to the people of Lystra (see above, p. 197). The other characteristic note of his preaching at Thessalonica was equally prominent in his speech at Athens. Here, as there (1 Thess. i. 10), the announcement of the judgment and the

---

[1] Bishop Lightfoot, *Biblical Essays*, p. 260.

proclamation of the raising of the future Judge from the dead by the Father are linked closely together. Further, it is important for our immediate purpose to notice how each element in this proclamation of the Gospel at Athens is Pauline. The season of judgment is, according to the imagery of the Old Testament (*e.g.* Am. v. 18, Is. ii. 12), described as "a day" (comp. *e.g.* 1 Thess. v. 2, 4, 2 Thess. i. 10, ii. 2, 1 Cor. i. 8, Rom. ii. 5, 16, Phil. i. 6, 10). This "day," however it may be unknown to men, has been fixed in the Divine counsels (compare the line of thought in 2 Thess. ii., Rom. xiii. 11 f.). The judgment will be universal (comp. Rom. ii. 16, iii. 6, 2 Tim. iv. 1), and righteous (comp. *e.g.* Rom. ii. 5, 2 Tim. iv. 8). It will be the judgment of God the Father ministered through (ἐν) Him whom He ordained (ὥρισεν) by the Resurrection (comp. Rom. ii. 16, διὰ Χρ. Ἰησοῦ: Rom. i. 4, τοῦ ὁρισθέντος . . . ἐξ ἀναστ. νεκρῶν). The mediator in the judgment is a man (ἀνδρί: comp. 1 Tim. ii. 5, Rom. v. 15, 1 Cor. xv. 47, Phil. ii. 7 f.).

At Lystra, as we saw, the speaker said nothing of his Christian message. At Athens the words which deal with distinctively Christian truths are few. And they are elementary. Christ is referred to simply as a man ($ἀνήρ$). The word is true, but it conveyed only half the truth about His Person. "Sic appellat Jesum," says Bengel, "pro captu auditorum. Plura erat dicturus audire cupientibus." The present was no fitting occasion to unfold the mystery of the Lord's divine glory. For when the listeners perceived that this strange teacher was speaking of the "resurrection of dead men," they jeered. Their own poet (Aesch. *Eum.* 647 f.), in the great assize-scene laid in that very Areopagus, had said,

> ἀνδρὸς δ'ἐπειδὰν αἷμ' ἀνασπάσῃ κόνις
> ἅπαξ θανόντος, οὕτις ἐστ' ἀνάστασις.

It was not worth their while to give him further hearing. "Solvuntur risu tabulae."

> Thou canst not think a mere barbarian Jew
> As Paulus proves to be, one circumcised,
> Hath access to a secret shut from us?
> Thou wrongest our philosophy, O king,
> In stooping to inquire of such an one,
> As if his answer could impose at all!

But some few had followed this "mere barbarian Jew" through the outer courts of natural religion to the threshold of the temple of revelation.

They had gained a glimpse, to use Bishop Butler's severely restrained phrase, of "the importance of Christianity."

Soon after the Apostle spoke these words on the Areopagus, he left Athens (xviii. 1). His success there was small. Only a few persons "clave unto him, and believed." There is, in the records of the Apostolic age, no evidence that a Christian community took root at Athens, or that St. Paul himself had any further communications with the little band of "brethren" there who owed their conversion to him. From Athens the Apostle passed on to Corinth. In the first Epistle to the Corinthians he reminds them how he came to them "in weakness, and in fear, and in much trembling" (ii. 3); how his preaching among them was free from all rhetorical art or recourse to human "wisdom" (ii. 1 ff.; comp. i. 18 ff., ii. 13); how that there "not many wise after the flesh . . . were called" (i. 26); how he had "determined not to know anything among [them] save Jesus Messiah, and him crucified" (ii. 2). We cannot but ask whether this deep depression and this emphatic assertion of the simplicity of the

Gospel were not prompted by some special circumstances. Was the Apostle conscious that at Athens he had for once been too eager to gain the "wise after the flesh," and that he had for this end gone far in the way of meeting philosophy with philosophy, and so had obscured the plain message of "a crucified Messiah" (1 Cor. i. 23)? If this is the true interpretation of his words in the Corinthian Epistle, we have a strong confirmation of the truthfulness of the historian's account of the Apostle's visit to Athens.

3. The last speech in the Acts with which we have to deal is the Pastoral Speech of St. Paul addressed to the Ephesian Elders at Miletus.

The speech at Miletus differs widely from all the other speeches contained in the Book. The latter are addressed either to "those without," whether Jews or Gentiles, or in one case (x. 34 ff.) to inquirers. In them a stranger speaks to strangers. In this one alone a Christian is represented as appealing to Christians, a chief pastor—and that chief pastor St. Paul—to the

Elders, to representative members, of a flock which he had long tended. The character of the speech then challenges and facilitates a comparison of its language and its ideas with the language and the ideas of St. Paul's Epistles. The line of thought is simple and direct; the tone is devotional, not didactic, still less controversial. One trait of the speech alone must at this point be noticed. In this Pauline speech, as in the Pauline Epistles, there are strong undercurrents, which interrupt the even flow of the tide. A topic is apparently dismissed; presently it forces its way into prominence again. The speech is primarily concerned with the past and the future. The pastor, in the midst of the pain of a present parting, recalls to his hearers' minds his life and work among them; he appeals to their remembrance of what he has been to them as a complete refutation of charges which have been, or may be, brought against his motives and against his teaching. He forecasts what the future has in store for himself and for the Church of Ephesus, and with these anticipations he connects his pastoral charge.

(1) The Past.

Thrice in the speech the Apostle is represented as appealing to the knowledge and the remembrance of his hearers (*vv.* 18, 31, 34). Such an appeal is eminently in the manner of St. Paul.[1] First he recalls to their minds his unbroken sojourn among them: "Ye yourselves know from the first day (comp. Phil. i. 5) that I set foot in Asia, how it was with you that I was the whole time" (πῶς μεθ' ὑμῶν τὸν πάντα χρόνον ἐγενόμην). The words—note the emphasis on "with you"—imply that during the whole of his visit to Asia he made Ephesus his home. This statement is in complete accord with an incidental notice in a letter of St. Paul to a neighbouring church (Col. ii. 1), from which we learn that neither the "brethren" at Colossæ nor those at Laodicea, nor—as the language seems to imply—others in that district of Asia, had ever "seen his face in the flesh." The assurance of his fervent prayers on behalf of all such [2]

---

[1] 1 Thess. ii. 1 f., 5, 11, iii. 4, iv. 2, 2 Thess. iii. 7, Gal. iv. 13. Phil. iv. 15 (knowledge); 2 Thess. ii. 5, 1 Cor. xi. 2, Eph. ii. 11 (remembrance); comp. *e.g.* 1 Thess. ii. 10, 1 Cor. iv. 17.

[2] θέλω γὰρ ὑμᾶς εἰδέναι, ἡλίκον ἀγῶνα ἔχω ὑπὲρ ὑμῶν καὶ τῶν ἐν Λ. καὶ ὅσοι οὐχ ἑόρακαν κ.τ.λ. (Col. ii. 1; comp. i. 3, iv. 12).

is doubtless intended to allay any feeling of resentment on their part, that he had long been near them and yet had never come to them. During those three years (*v.* 31) then the disciples at Ephesus had been able narrowly to watch their teacher's life and work.

They had seen his life. It was a life of continuous bond-service to his Master (δουλεύων τῷ κυρίῳ : comp. *e.g.* Rom. xii. 11, Phil. ii. 22, Eph. vi. 7 ; Rom. i. 1, Gal. vi. 17). They had been witnesses of all that that service involved —" with all lowliness of mind (comp. Eph. iv. 2 ; and *e.g.* 1 Thess. ii. 6 ff., 2 Cor. iv. 5, vii. 6), and with tears (comp. *v.* 31, 2 Cor. ii. 4, Phil. iii. 18 ; and *e.g.* 1 Cor. ii. 3, 2 Cor. i. 8, Rom. ix. 2), and with trials which befell me by the plots of the Jews." The Apostle's ministry at Ephesus was saddened by personal sorrows and by the hostility of enemies,— " without were fightings, within were fears" (2 Cor. vii. 5). In St. Luke's narrative of the events at Ephesus, though there is a hint of the opposition of the Jews (xix. 9), the foreground of the picture is filled with the stirring scenes of the trade riot, in which Demetrius the silversmith is the ringleader.

In the First Epistle to the Corinthians, written at Ephesus (xvi. 8), there are brief but significant allusions to opposition of many kinds —"There are many adversaries" (xvi. 9); and to some signal crisis of personal violence—"If after the manner of men I fought with beasts at Ephesus" (xv. 32). In the latter passage the reference can hardly be to the tumult in the theatre; for (1) the Apostle, when he wrote the letter, was contemplating a further sojourn at Ephesus (xvi. 8), and this he could hardly have done after that violent outburst; indeed, in the Acts, our one authority for the story of the proceedings of Demetrius and his fellow-craftsmen, we are expressly told that he left Ephesus immediately "after the uproar was ceased"; (2) we learn from the Acts that the advice of his friends and the warning of the Asiarchs restrained St. Paul from "adventuring himself into the theatre" (xix. 30 f.), so that he himself did not come into contact with the infuriated mob. The words, then, in 1 Cor. xv. 32 must allude to some earlier peril (comp. Rom. xvi. 4,

Acts xviii. 26), and we may not unreasonably connect them with "the plots of the Jews" mentioned in the speech. It is clear, however, that these "plots" were something much more to the Apostle than harassing dangers; they involved "temptations." It is in reference to this period that St. Paul tells the Corinthian disciples "concerning our affliction which befell us in Asia, that we were weighed down exceedingly, beyond our power, insomuch that we despaired even of life" (2 Cor. i. 8). Why these outward perils overwhelmed him with bitter sorrow, and even brought with them spiritual trials, is made plain in the Epistle to the Romans, an Epistle written apparently at Corinth just before the Apostle started on this last journey to Jerusalem (Acts xx. 2 f.). That letter reveals St. Paul's yearning love for his countrymen and his deep conviction that the divine counsels with regard to them were permanent and inviolable. The persevering treachery, then, with which the Jews dogged his steps, for no other reason than because he was the herald of the Messiah, tested not only his courage and his patience but also his faith in the God of Israel. "The plots of the Jews" brought St. Paul face to face with the dark problem of Israel's unbelief in a concrete and personal form. The Apostle's wrestling with these "temptations," these subtle assailants of the calm assurance of his faith, was a spectacle on which, at least in part, the Ephesian Elders had looked.

St. Paul's work also—his method and the substance of his teaching—was known to the Ephesians—"Teaching you publicly, and from house to house, testifying both to Jews and to Greeks repentance toward God, and faith toward our Lord Jesus Christ" (*vv.* 20 f.). If these words were really (in substance) spoken by St. Paul, they give a vivid picture of the Apostle's ministry at one of the great churches which he founded—a picture more vivid, perhaps, and more comprehensive than any we find elsewhere. He "used both public and private monitions and exhortations." On the one hand, the speaker recalls to the Elders how he had been constant in giving instruction in the assemblies of "the Brethren." The allusions in the Epistles to such public teaching are indirect. Such a habit on the Apostle's part is implied when he refers to exhortations given to his correspondents while he was yet with them (2 Thess. iii. 10, 1 Cor. xi. 23, xv. 1), and when he gives directions as to the due conduct of assemblies for worship and instruction (1 Cor. xiv. 18 f.). The public reading of his Epistles, when he himself was absent, was clearly meant to take the place of his personal public utterances (1 Thess. v. 27, Col. iv. 16). And indeed a statement as to so obvious an element in the work of an Apostle is self-evidently true and natural. On the other hand, the Elders knew how diligent the Apostle had been in dealing with individuals. The house-to-house visitation of the persecutor (κατὰ τοὺς οἴκους εἰσπορευόμενος, Acts viii. 3) had passed into the house-to-house visitation of the Christian pastor (κατ' οἴκους, xx. 20). In regard to this matter also, the Epistles supply no precise parallel. In them no reference is ever made in definite terms to St. Paul's work in the homes of inquirers or of disciples; but the Apostle's sense of responsibility for individuals is in different ways emphasized again and again.

Two passages, for example,—the one in his earliest Epistle, the other in one of the Epistles of the first Roman captivity,—sufficiently prove the earnestness and the tenderness with which he dealt with individuals: "Ye know how we dealt with each one of you, as a father with his own children, exhorting you, and encouraging you" (1 Thess. ii. 11); "Admonishing every man and teaching every man in all wisdom, that we may present every man perfect in Christ" (Col. i. 28). The thought and the language of these passages—the "each one of you" of the former of them, and the thrice-repeated "every man" of the latter—are very closely akin to the thought and the language of some of the closing words of the speech: "By the space of three years I ceased not to admonish every one night and day with tears" (*v.* 31). It is sufficient simply to notice the other details of the ministry at Ephesus — its comprehensiveness, "testifying both to Jews and Greeks" (comp. 1 Cor. i. 24 ff., xii. 13, Rom. i. 14 ff., iii. 9, x. 12); and its twofold message, "repentance toward God (comp. *e.g.* 2 Cor. v. 20 ff.), and faith toward our Lord Jesus Christ" (comp. *e.g.* Rom. x. 9 ff.).

(2) The Apologia.

The leader of a great movement is commonly indifferent, at least outwardly, to praise or blame. He presses on with the work of the present, and leaves the calumnies of enemies and the complaints of half-hearted friends to that final court of appeal, the long lapse of time. If he is a religious man, his thoughts rise higher, to God who knows all hearts and who will in the end vindicate His servant. Such at times was St. Paul's feeling: "With me it is a very small thing that I should be judged of you, or of man's judgment: yea, I judge not mine own self. . . . He that judgeth me is the Lord" (1 Cor. iv. 3 f.). But it was not always so with him. His Epistles reveal him to us as a man of keen sensibility, whose heart was too tender and too impetuous not to be irritated beyond the possibility of a calm silence by the open charges and the whispered insinuations of overt adversaries and of false allies. Moreover, a nobler influence was at work than the mere impulses of natural character. St. Paul never doubted that he had received his call as an Apostle from the Lord Jesus himself. Such an apostleship must be above suspicion. "That the ministry be not blamed" was the true motive of very much of St. Paul's uncompromising self-assertion. The personal and the official character of the Apostle alike made it impossible for him contentedly to forget slanders, however unscrupulous and unfounded, of which he was the victim. We trace, especially in the letters which belong to the active period of his life, a habit of self-defence, persistent, eager, at times almost fierce in its intensity. He meets a charge; when he has passed from it, the painful recollection haunts him and insensibly moulds his treatment of other matters; presently he returns to the slander, and again refutes it. That this is a true statement of the case will be plain to any sympathetic student of the two Epistles to the Thessalonians, and especially of the Second Epistle to the Corinthians. The latter Epistle more than any other reveals the heart of St. Paul; in it he lays bare to his readers a conflict of contending emotions, and all through the letter a dominating element is that of *apologia*. This letter, it will be observed, was written shortly after St. Paul's long sojourn at Ephesus ended (xx. 1 f.), and so within a few months of this leave-taking at Miletus. In the speech at Miletus we note precisely the same apologetic spirit at work as we trace in these Epistles. At certain points it finds clear and definite expression (*vv.* 26, 33). All through the speech its influence is not far from the surface; it inspires the appeal to the Elders' intimate knowledge of St. Paul's life, and the reference to his supreme ambition of "fulfilling . . . the ministry which I received from the Lord Jesus "(*v.* 24). And further, after the solemn and pathetic words of commendation (*v.* 32), which were intended, as it would seem likely, to close the speech, we have one of those swift retrogressions and revulsions of feeling by which we are sometimes startled in St. Paul's Epistles (comp. *e.g.* 2 Cor. vi. 11–vii. 4, Phil. iii. 1 f.), and the speaker abruptly and prosaically returns to the same theme of self-defence: " I coveted no man's silver, or gold, or apparel" (*v.* 33).

When we ask the question — From what charges and insinuations was St. Paul so anxious to defend himself? — the answer is supplied by a typical passage in his earliest Epistle: "Our exhortation is not of error, nor of uncleanness, nor in guile; but even as we have been approved of God to be intrusted with the gospel, so we speak; not as pleasing men, but God which proveth our hearts. For neither at any time were we found using words of flattery, as ye know, nor a cloke of covetousness ($\pi\lambda\epsilon o\nu\epsilon\xi\iota\alpha\varsigma$), God is witness; nor seeking glory of men, neither from you, nor from others, when we might have been burdensome ($\delta\upsilon\nu\acute{a}\mu\epsilon\nu o\iota\ \acute{\epsilon}\nu\ \beta\acute{a}\rho\epsilon\iota\ \epsilon\hat{\iota}\nu\alpha\iota$), as apostles of Christ. . . . For ye remember, brethren, our labour and travail: working night and day, that we might not burden ($\pi\rho\grave{o}\varsigma\ \tau\grave{o}\ \mu\grave{\eta}\ \acute{\epsilon}\pi\iota\beta\alpha\rho\hat{\eta}\sigma\alpha\iota$) any of you, we preached unto you the gospel of God. Ye are witnesses, and God also, how holily and righteously and unblameably we behaved ourselves towards you that believe" (1 Thess. ii. 3 ff.).

The charges at which the Apostle here hints are, to speak broadly, two. (i) His motives were impugned. He was dominated, it was said, by a lust for power and influence. He aimed at gaining a personal ascendancy over his converts. Or, as others seem to have alleged, his designs were simply mercenary. His ministry was a mere matter of money, an expedient for enriching himself at the expense of his enthusiastic followers. (ii) His faithfulness as an evangelist and teacher was called in question. His preaching was no simple and sincere proclamation of the Gospel. It was limited and moulded by his own selfish designs. To win popularity he must needs play the time-server and the flatterer.

Both these charges are in St. Paul's mind in other passages of his Epistles, and they are met in the words of the speech.

(i) To the accusation of self-seeking, so far as it involved an imputation of compassing undue authority and influence (comp. 2 Cor. i. 24, iv. 5, x. 1 ff.), there is probably an indirect reference in the words: "I hold not my life of any account (comp. Phil. ii. 30), as dear unto myself, so that I may accomplish my course (comp. 2 Tim. iv. 7), and the ministry (comp.

Col. iv. 17, 2 Tim. iv. 5, Col. i. 25; and *e.g.* 2 Cor. iii. 6, iv. 1, v. 18) which I received from the Lord Jesus (comp. Gal. i. 1, 12, 1 Tim. i. 12), to declare ($\delta\iota\alpha\mu\alpha\rho\tau\acute{\nu}\rho\alpha\sigma\theta\alpha\iota$, comp. 1 Thess. iv. 6) the gospel of the grace of God" (God's free benevolence towards all men; comp. Rom. v. 15 ff., 2 Cor. vi. 1, Eph. i. 7, ii. 7, iii. 2, Col. i. 6). In the Epistles this surrender on the Apostle's part of life and of the joy of living for the sake of Christ and His work finds frequent expression in different contexts; see *e.g.* 2 Cor. iv. 7 ff., vi. 4 ff., xii. 9 f., Phil. i. 20, iii. 8, Col. i. 24. It is a subject which, especially in the Second Epistle to Corinth, is seldom far from his thoughts, and, when it forces itself into prominence, it breaks down the barriers of natural reticence and even of Christian humility. No one, his words to the Ephesian Elders seem to imply, who so freely gave himself up for his work's sake could in that work be seeking the glory of self. But a more ready weapon against the Apostle was supplied by the insinuation that money was his real quest. This was an accusation which all could understand. His "defence" to those who at Corinth constituted themselves his inquisitors was the assertion of his right as an Apostle to earn his livelihood, coupled with the assurance that he had in relation to the Corinthians voluntarily foregone the exercise of that right (1 Cor. ix. 3-18; comp. 2 Cor. xi. 7 ff., xii. 13). But his very defence, it seems not unlikely, was converted into evidence against him. Somehow supplies came to him. It is possible that his own strong phrase, "I robbed ($\dot{\epsilon}\sigma\acute{\upsilon}\lambda\eta\sigma\alpha$) other churches" (2 Cor. xi. 8), is in reality an echo of the random charges flung at him at Corinth. The Apostle's earliest and simplest reply to his adversaries was the fact that "night and day" he worked at the trade which he had learned for his own support. With his words already quoted from the First Epistle to the Thessalonians we compare a passage from the Second Epistle to that church: "Yourselves know how ye ought to imitate us: for we behaved not ourselves disorderly among you; neither did we eat bread for nought at any man's hand, but in labour and travail, working night and day, that we might not burden any of you: not because we have not the right, but to make ourselves an ensample unto you, that ye should imitate us" (2 Thess. iii. 7 ff.). When to these two passages from St. Paul's two earliest letters we add another from a later Epistle—"Let him that stole steal no more: but rather let him labour, working with his hands the thing that is good, *that he may have whereof to give to him that hath need*" (Eph. iv. 28)—we have the three ideas presented in the words of the Pauline speech: "I coveted no man's silver, or gold, or apparel. Ye yourselves know that these hands ministered unto my necessities, and to them that were with me. In all things I gave you an example, how that so labouring, ye ought to help the weak" (*vv.* 33 ff.). These ideas are — (1) the Apostle's own strenuous activity in manual work; (2) the example which he thereby set before his own converts; (3) the fruitfulness of such labour in the power it gave to succour the needy. The duty of the Christian man "to shew himself gentle, and to be merciful for Christ's sake to poor and needy people," was, as is clear from the Epistles written in the immediately preceding period, prominent in St. Paul's thoughts at this time—

"Bear ye one another's burdens, and so fulfil the law of Christ" (Gal. vi. 2); "We that are strong ought to bear the infirmities of the weak, and not to please ourselves" (Rom. xv. 1; comp. 1 Thess. v. 14). Indeed his present journey to Jerusalem with all its inevitable dangers had been undertaken for the express purpose of bringing to "the poor among the saints that [were] at Jerusalem" the gifts of the richer churches in Macedonia and Achaia (Rom. xv. 26). With the fulfilment of this Christian duty the Apostle is represented in the speech as connecting the constant remembrance of "the words of the Lord Jesus, how he himself said, It is more blessed to give than to receive" (Acts xx. 35). In precisely the same spirit, writing to the Galatians, St. Paul insists on brotherly sympathy and help as a fulfilment of "the law of the Christ" (vi. 2), the law which the Christ enforced by His express words (John xiii. 34) and by His life and death; and in the Epistle to the Romans the decisive plea for unselfish service of others lies in that same divine example—"For the Christ also pleased not himself" (xv. 3). In the Pauline speech a saying of the Lord's is adduced, a saying which has not been recorded in our Gospels. The speaker quotes it as already familiar to his hearers, and we cannot but infer that the teaching of Christ had been a subject on which he had instructed his friends when he was living among them. Such a conclusion is altogether in harmony with the evidence of the Epistles of St. Paul. Many "oracles of the Lord" may be imbedded in the Apostle's writings, which, as they have no place in the Gospels, it is impossible now to identify; but an important series of coincidences with the text of our Gospels is contained in the Pauline Epistles.[1] Further, in the First Epistle to the Corinthians he appeals explicitly to a commandment of "the Lord" as decisive on the question of divorce (vii. 10; comp. *vv.* 12, 25), and in one of his latest Epistles (1 Tim. vi. 3; comp. 1 Tim. v. 18, Luke x. 7) he appears to refer to a collection of the "words of our Lord Jesus Christ," whether oral or written. It is therefore quite natural that he should recall to his

---

[1] I have collected many of these coincidences in *The Lord's Prayer in the Early Church* (Texts and Studies, i. 3), pp. 19 ff.

hearers one of "the wholesome words" of the Lord Jesus, that it might remain ever printed in their remembrance.

(ii) Closely related to this charge of obedience to selfish and sordid aims, which drew from the Apostle the appeal to his industry as a craftsman, was the charge of unfaithfulness to the truth which he had been commissioned to proclaim. The gospel of the self-seeker must needs be "words of flattery" (1 Thess. ii. 5). St. Paul discovered that to speak the truth sometimes in the view of his converts transformed him into an enemy (Gal. iv. 16). To this imputation of unfaithfulness St. Paul refers, as we have seen, in his earliest extant letter. He meets it again with an emphatic plea of "not guilty" in the Second Epistle to the Corinthians: "We are not as the many, playing the huckster with the word of God (καπηλεύοντες τὸν λόγον τοῦ θεοῦ): but as of sincerity, but as of God, in the sight of God, speak we in Christ" (ii. 17); and again, "We have renounced the hidden things of shame, not walking in craftiness, nor adulterating (δολοῦντες) the word of God; but by manifestation of the truth commending ourselves to every man's conscience in the sight of God. But and if our gospel is veiled, it is veiled in them that are perishing" (iv. 2 ff.). In both passages the figure is drawn from the sale of wine; but the metaphor in the former passage is more comprehensive, and includes that of the latter. The huckster too often, for the sake of gain, adulterates his goods and gives scant measure to the buyer. So the teacher who is bent on his own advantage mingles with his message soft and cozening words, and is silent as to all difficult and unwelcome truths. Such, St. Paul asserts, was not his character. In his ministry and in his gospel there was no element of falseness. He won men by unfolding to them "the truth," the truth in all its entirety. If his gospel failed, it failed only in the case of those whose rescue from death lay beyond his power. It is plain at once how closely related to the protestations of the speech are these protestations of the Epistle. There is no similarity between them in language, but the main ideas are the same: "I shrank not from declaring unto you anything that was profitable" (οὐδὲν ὑπεστειλάμην τῶν

συμφερόντων τοῦ μὴ ἀναγγεῖλαι ὑμῖν, v. 20). . . .
"I testify unto you this day that I am pure from the blood of all men. For I shrank not from declaring unto you the whole counsel of God" (οὐ γὰρ ὑπεστειλάμην τοῦ μὴ ἀναγγεῖλαι πᾶσαν τὴν βουλὴν τοῦ θεοῦ ὑμῖν, vv. 26 f.). The speaker protests that all that he could do has been done. The guilt of spiritual murder, the curse and condemnation of every teacher who is swayed by worldly aims, does not rest on him. The repeated "I shrank not from declaring unto you" emphasizes the assurance that he had suppressed nothing from fear or favour, nothing of that which was "profitable," nothing of "the whole counsel of God." That latter phrase (comp. Eph. i. 11, τοῦ τὰ πάντα ἐνεργοῦντος κατὰ τὴν βουλὴν τοῦ θελήματος αὐτοῦ) points to the divine policy, if the word may be allowed, in the creation and redemption of man, God's "good pleasure which he purposed in [Christ] unto a dispensation of the fulness of the seasons" (Eph. i. 9 f.). On the one side, this unfolding to the Ephesian Church of "the whole counsel of God" included in its scope the spiritual "wisdom" which St. Paul says that he

"spoke among the full-grown," "the wisdom that hath been hidden, which God foreordained before the worlds unto our glory" (1 Cor. ii. 6 ff.). On the other hand, it involved insistence on holiness of heart and life as the necessary corollary to be drawn from the historic facts of Christ's death, resurrection, and exaltation—the believer's death unto sin and his new birth unto righteousness (comp. Rom. vi. 2 ff., Col. iii. 1 ff., Eph. ii. 4 ff., iv. 20 ff.)—"This is the will of God, even your sanctification" (1 Thess. iv. 3). Further, the other phrase, "the things that are profitable" (τὰ συμφέροντα), points to the ethical and social application of the Gospel to the problems of daily life—complete abstinence from all the contaminating influences of surrounding idolatry (comp. *e.g.* 1 Cor. x. 14 ff.; 2 Cor. vi. 14 ff.), the "walking in wisdom toward them that are without" (Col. iv. 5), family duties (Col. iii. 18 ff., Eph. v. 22), the obligation of following "honest occupations," which were "good and profitable unto men" (Titus iii. 8). The brief phrases of the speech then are seen to summarize the detailed teaching of the Epistles. The Apostle's defence is that neither by the promptings of avarice nor by the desire for popularity had he been seduced into silence as to either the verities of the Gospel or its bearing on conduct.

(3) The Forecast of the Future.

The Apostle is represented in the speech as looking beyond the present moment and steadily fixing his gaze on the horizon. Through the mists of uncertainty he discerns both for the Ephesian Church and for himself lowering clouds.

(1) His anticipation for himself is given in the words : "And now, behold, I go bound in the spirit unto Jerusalem, not knowing the things that shall befall me there : save that the Holy Ghost testifieth unto me in every city, saying that bonds and afflictions abide me. But I hold not my life of any account, as dear unto myself. . . . And now, behold, I know that ye all, among whom I went about preaching the kingdom, shall see my face no more" (*vv.* 22 ff.). In regard to three points we compare these words with passages from St. Paul's Epistles.

(*a*) The journey to Jerusalem here referred to was no sudden resolve. Months before, when the Apostle wrote from Ephesus to the Corinthians, a collection on behalf of the poorer Brethren at Jerusalem was already in progress (1 Cor. xvi. 1 ff.), and it then seemed possible that it might be right for St. Paul himself to go to Jerusalem with the gift (*v.* 4). As time went on his purpose became fixed. He realized that it was a matter of the last importance for the binding together of the Jewish Churches of Palestine and the Churches of the Gentile world that he himself, the Apostle of the Gentiles, should be the bearer of this liberality of the Gentiles, and should himself be witness of what he hoped would be the joyful acceptance of these gifts on the part of the Jewish Christians. When he wrote from Corinth to the Roman Church his mind was already made up—"Now I go unto Jerusalem, ministering unto the saints" (Rom. xv. 25). But with the conviction that the journey was necessary, there grew up an assurance that it could only be carried out at the risk of his life. With unusual earnestness and solemnity he asks for the prayers of the Christians at Rome, both that he may be brought safely through the days of peril, and that a

happy issue may crown his efforts after peace—
"Now I beseech you, brethren, by our Lord
Jesus Christ, and by the love of the Spirit, that
ye wrestle together with me in your prayers to
God for me; that I may be delivered from them
that are disobedient in Judæa, and that my
ministration which I have for Jerusalem may
be acceptable to the saints; that I may come
unto you in joy through the will of God, and
together with you find rest" (Rom. xv. 30 ff.). In
this forecast, serious as the danger seemed, hope
on the whole predominates. The Apostle's
plans are allowed to extend beyond the visit to
the Holy City; he looks forward with some
confidence to visiting Rome. If with the sober
hopefulness of the Epistle we contrast the tone
of unselfish and tender submissiveness which
pervades the speech, yet, when we look beneath
the surface, we perceive that the difference of
feeling is quite natural. The sense that he was
parting from dear friends could not but deepen
for St. Paul the gloom which hung over his
future. The mind at such a moment cannot
brace itself to hope. Moreover, from an incidental notice in the Acts we learn that, since

he wrote to the Roman Church, he had been obliged to change his route because of a plot of the Jews (Acts xx. 3). If such were the dangers which surrounded him in a distant colony of the Dispersion, what would be likely to happen in Jerusalem, where Jewish malice and cunning were at their strongest, and where "the restraining power" of the Roman authorities would be least anxious to assert itself? The picture, then, which the author of the Acts draws of St. Paul's attitude towards his journey to Jerusalem is in itself natural; moreover, its truthfulness is confirmed by incidental notices alike in the Epistles and in the Book of the Acts itself.

(*b*) In two points we note a divergence between the Epistles and the speech.

(i) It appears from the Epistles to the Corinthians and the Romans, that St. Paul's mind was full of the act of liberality which was the occasion of his journey. The two things—his journey and his mission as the almoner of the Gentile Churches—were bound up together in his thoughts. Nothing, however, in the speech is said in reference to the collection for the "poor saints" at Jerusalem. It is quite possible that the omission is illusory; a reference to the subject contained in the actual address may well have dropped out in the condensed report. But, on the other hand, such silence on the Apostle's part may have been deliberate. The Churches of Galatia, Macedonia, and Achaia are explicitly mentioned in the Epistles as sharing in the gift sent by St. Paul's hands to Jerusalem (1 Cor. xvi. 1, 2 Cor. viii. 1 ff., Rom. xv. 26). If we may argue from the absence in the Epistles of any mention of the Churches of Asia in this connexion, we conclude that these churches, for whatever reason, had taken no part in this benevolent work. If this was so, then we may well believe that, when it was now too late for them to give him assistance in the work which he had so much at heart, delicacy of feeling prevented the Apostle from blazoning before his Ephesian friends the generosity of other churches. But, though no mention of the collection is found in the speech, the overwhelming sense of obligation and duty which we know that St. Paul felt in regard to it finds expression in the significant phrase: "And now, behold, I go bound in the spirit unto Jerusalem" (*v.* 22). From the speech as much as from the Epistles we gather that in this journey to Jerusalem St. Paul held that he was simply doing what he could, in the whole range of its responsibilities, to "accomplish the ministry which [he had] received from the Lord Jesus" (*v.* 24).

(ii) The Apostle is here (*v.* 25) represented as expressing his own strong conviction (ἐγὼ οἶδα) that he will never see his beloved converts again; this is their last meeting on earth. If, however, as I believe that we are justified in doing, we accept as genuine the Pastoral Epistles, it seems clear that, after his first Roman captivity was over, St. Paul did revisit Ephesus. This at least is the most natural interpretation of his words to Timothy, "I exhorted thee to tarry at Ephesus, when I was going into Macedonia" (1 Tim. i. 3), and of his reference in his last Epistle (2 Tim. i. 15 ff.) to the defection from him of "all that are in Asia" contrasted with the faithful ministration to him at Ephesus on the part of Onesiphorus. In any case, even if this interpretation of these particular words is questioned, or if the authenticity of these

Epistles is denied, these passages represent an early tradition that the Apostle was brought safely through his perils and regained his liberty. Though it is not legitimate to lay too much stress on such an argument, yet it seems unlikely that a romancer would have put into the Apostle's mouth a series of prophecies which an early tradition about the Apostle's later history represented as mistaken.

(c) The language of the speech in reference to the Apostle's death is very closely akin to his words on this subject in the Epistle to the Philippians (i. 21-26). There is the same solemnity, the same calmness, of tone; the same contentment with the sterner issue, if that should come; the same instinctive anxiety to forget himself and to review the possibilities of the future in their relation to the Apostle's work and in their relation to his friends. Moreover, one word—commonly misinterpreted—reveals the same conception of death which is characteristic of some notable passages in the Epistles. The Apostle speaks (v. 29) of what will happen to his friends μετὰ τὴν ἄφιξίν μου, "after my arrival," "after my long journey is over and

I have reached my true home.[1]" The contrast which is thus suggested enhances the significance of the words—his fellow-workers will be in peril; the Apostle himself will be at rest in the presence of his Lord. We compare St. Paul's words to the Philippians: "I am in a strait betwixt the two, having the desire to depart and *be with Christ* . . . yet to abide in the flesh is more needful for your sake" (i. 23 f.). A still closer parallel is supplied by the Apostle's language in an earlier Epistle about being "absent from the Lord" (ἐκδημοῦμεν ἀπὸ τοῦ κυρίου) during the life on earth, and after the death of the body being "present with the Lord" (ἐνδημῆσαι πρὸς τὸν κύριον, 2 Cor. v. 6 ff.). The ἄφιξις of the speech and the ἐκδημῆσαι and ἐνδημῆσαι of the Epistle form a group of words in which the present life is regarded as a journey or as a sojourn in an alien region, and

---

[1] Such is the regular meaning of ἄφιξις (comp. ἀφικνεῖσθαι) from Herodotus (*e.g.* i. 69, vii. 58, ix. 76) onwards. Compare 3 Macc. vii. 18, τοῦ βασιλέως χορηγήσαντος αὐτοῖς εὐψύχως τὰ πρὸς τὴν ἄφιξιν πάντα ἑκάστῳ ἕως ἐπὶ τὴν ἰδίαν οἰκίαν: Joseph. *Ant.* IV. viii. 47, πρὸς τοὺς ἡμετέρους ἄπειμι προγόνους καὶ θεὸς τήνδε μοι τὴν ἡμέραν τῆς πρὸς ἐκείνους ἀφίξεως ὥρισε. It is not impossible that the phrase in the Acts is an abbreviation of a fuller phrase (actually used in the speech) such as μετὰ τὴν πρὸς τὸν κύριον ἄφιξίν μου.

death the entrance into that Presence which is the spirit's true home.

(II) The Apostle is represented, as we have already seen, as connecting together his own future and the future of his converts. The prospect was dark for them, as (from an earthly standpoint) it was for him. "I know (comp. Phil. i. 19, 25) that after my arrival home grievous wolves shall enter in among you, not sparing the flock; and from among your own selves shall men arise, speaking perverted things, to draw away the disciples after them" *vv.* 29 f.). The Ephesians are warned of a twofold peril.

(i) Dangers would assail them from without. Persecutors would do their pitiless worst against the Church. Such appears to be the natural interpretation of the metaphor of the wolves and the flock (2 Esdras v. 18, Enoch lxxxix. 13 ff.; Matt. x. 16 ‖ Luke x. 3, John x. 12). That the sufferings which, for Christ's sake, his converts endured touched St. Paul's heart is clear from his Epistles (1 Thess. ii. 14 ff., iii. 1 ff., 2 Thess. i. 4, Phil. i. 29). Years before this time he had taken pains to forearm his friends at Thessalonica against such troubles, and against the temptations which they would inevitably bring with them (1 Thess. iii. 4). But here the Apostle's forecast is no mere general prophecy of persecution—"all that would live godly in Christ Jesus shall suffer persecution" (2 Tim. iii. 12). He appears to discern signs of some definite and particular storm of persecution which will be the sequel of his own death—his own violent death. If we endeavour to penetrate beneath the surface of St. Paul's words, we may reasonably suppose that his thoughts went back to the past. The death of the first martyr kindled the fury of Saul the Pharisee, and "there arose on that day a great persecution against the church which was at Jerusalem" (Acts viii. 1). Nay, he could not but remember that his madness against these hated Nazarenes goaded him to "persecute them even unto foreign cities" (Acts xxvi. 11). History would repeat itself. When the Apostle himself, as he expected, fell a victim to "the plots of the Jews" at Jerusalem, he may well have thought that the infection of their victorious hatred would extend to the Dispersion, and that the Jews, in the cities where they were strong in number and influence, possibly in alliance with the interested fanaticism of such men as Demetrius and his fellow-craftsmen, would lead a crusade against the Christian Church. Perhaps the Apostle felt that the crisis was at hand, of which he had written to the Thessalonians (2 Thess. ii.), when "the restraining power"—the authority of the Roman magistracy—keeping down these dangerous ebullitions of Jewish feeling (comp. Acts xviii. 12 ff.), would, for whatever cause, be withdrawn. The details of the vision of this troubled future, as it rose before St. Paul's mind, it is impossible to restore with certainty. It must be enough that it has points of contact with the Apostle's earlier history and with his earlier anticipations of the triumph of Jewish violence.

(ii) But serious as the troubles would be which came from without, those which sprang from within would be even yet more full of peril. The persecutor is often the forerunner of the false teacher. There was a real danger lest the Ephesian Christians should be "led astray in the midst of these afflictions" (σαίνεσθαι ἐν ταῖς θλίψεσιν ταύταις, 1 Thess. iii. 3[1]); lest, in the tension and in the strain on the moral and spiritual powers which persecution would bring, the infant Church at Ephesus would fall a prey to the interested preachers of a gospel less simple and less exacting than that of St. Paul. Doubtless, when the Apostle warned the Elders —"from among your own selves shall men arise, speaking perverted things, to draw away the disciples after them" (*v.* 30)—he already saw symptoms of the disease which soon after broke out in the Asiatic Churches, "the philosophy and vain deceit" with which the Epistle to the Colossians deals (ii. 8), a disease to the ravages of which in a more virulent form the Apostle, writing at a later period, looked forward with increased dread (comp. *e.g.* 1 Tim. iv. 1, 2 Tim. iii. 13). Two points in the description of these errors stand out. (*a*) The false teachers would speak "perverted things" (διεστραμμένα). The Apostle is here represented as alleging, not that their doctrines would be wholly and absolutely false, but rather that in their hands Christian truth would be warped, and the proportion of its

---

[1] See Bishop Lightfoot's note *in loco.*

different elements lost. Such appears to be the character of the system of teaching impugned in the Epistle to the Colossians. That system did not so much involve a denial of the central truths of Christianity as lay a wholly undue stress on human "traditions" and on elementary precepts. St. Paul does not stigmatize it, as he stigmatized the teaching which had leavened the Galatian Church, as a gospel "different" from his own (Gal. i. 6). Such, too, was certainly the character of the errors which the Apostle had in view in the Pastoral Epistles. "The duty laid on Timothy and Titus is not to refute deadly errors, but to keep themselves clear, and to warn others to keep themselves clear, of *trivialities* which took the place of true religion." He condemned such teachings as "trashy and unwholesome stuff.[1]" (β) And in the second place the motives of these false guides would be on the same low and earthly level as their doctrine. Their ambition would be "to draw away the disciples after themselves" —"a simplicitate erga Christum et ab unitate

[1] I have ventured to quote two sentences from my notes of Dr. Hort's lectures on the Pastoral Epistles.

corporis" (Bengel). They would abuse the gift of personal influence, and exalt a following of themselves into a standard and test of faith. Of such a degradation of the pastoral office the Epistles reveal St. Paul's habitual dread and condemnation. Thus, at the close of the almost contemporary Epistle to the Romans, the Apostle suddenly digresses into a vehement warning: "Now I beseech you, brethren, mark them which are causing the divisions and occasions of stumbling, contrary to the doctrine which ye learned: and turn away from them. For they that are such serve not our Lord Christ, but their own belly; and by their smooth and fair speech they beguile the hearts of the innocent" (xvi. 17 f.). In the later Epistle to the Colossians a similar note of caution is sounded in the words: "Take heed lest there shall be any one that maketh spoil of you" (ὁ συλαγωγῶν, ii. 8). And in the Pastoral Epistles we compare the painful picture of those "that creep into houses, and take captive (αἰχμαλωτίζοντες) silly women laden with sins" (2 Tim. iii. 6), and the instructions given to Titus (iii. 10) as to the treatment of "a man that is factious" (αἱρετικὸν ἄνθρωπον; comp. 2 Tim. iv. 14, Titus i. 11). It is clear that St. Paul, as time passed on, was keenly alive to the danger lest on the one hand the simplicity of the Gospel should be corrupted and its exacting strictness relaxed, and lest on the other hand personal discipleship to some designing teacher of this lower type should in the minds of his converts take the place of membership in the Church of Christ (comp. 1 Cor. i. 11 ff., iii. 21 f., iv. 6 f.). The warning which he is represented in the Acts as urging on the Ephesian Elders is wholly in keeping with what the Epistles disclose as to his habitual anxiety on the subject.

(4) The Pastoral Charge and Commendation.

The Apostle is represented as passing at once from the assertion of his own pastoral innocence to the ideal of life and service which he sets before the Elders: "Take heed unto yourselves (προσέχετε ἑαυτοῖς) and to all the flock" (v. 28). To the phrase itself, and to this insistence on self-discipline as the primary obligation which rests on the "shepherd of souls," there is a close parallel in St. Paul's charge to Timothy: "Take heed to thyself (ἔπεχε σεαυτῷ), and to thy teaching. Continue in these things; for in doing this thou shalt save both thyself and them that hear thee" (1 Tim. iv. 16). The flock will be rightly tended only by the pastor who as a first duty tends himself. Stress is doubtless laid on the "all"—"take heed unto *all* the flock." The warning against the intrusion into the work of the ministry of the spirit of partiality—the partiality which would, for example, neglect the Jewish Christians, and be at pains only to meet the spiritual needs of the converts from idolatry — is entirely Pauline. In the Epistles, to refer only to one instance of St. Paul's habitual thought, the Apostle again and again emphasizes the fact that his words are addressed to, and that his affections are warm towards, "you all" (1 Thess. i. 2, 2 Thess. iii. 18, 2 Cor. i. 1, ii. 3, vii. 13, 15, xiii. 13, Rom. i. 8, Phil. i. 1, 4, 7, 8, ii. 17; comp. Col. i. 28). The true pastor must recognize the oneness of the flock, and the need of nurture and of care which belongs to each member of it.

The duties of the pastoral office are described

in the light of its source and of its essential character.

The source whence the Ephesian Elders derived their office was the Holy Ghost—"in the which the Holy Ghost set you as overseers" (*v.* 28). The language used certainly does not exclude the possibility that they may have been chosen by the voice of the Church, and may have received their commission through the laying on of hands (vi. 3, xiv. 23, 1 Tim. iv. 14, 2 Tim. i. 6). But behind any human choice, behind any human act of ordination, there lay the divine action and will. Like Archippus at Colossæ, these Elders must "take heed to" a ministry which they had "received *in the Lord*" (Col. iv. 17). They were members of the flock; but "in" the flock, in the organism of the Church, they had, by divine appointment and through the divine working, a special and peculiar place as "overseers" (ἐν ᾧ ὑμᾶς τὸ πνεῦμα τὸ ἅγιον ἔθετο ἐπισκόπους). What is here said of a particular group of Elders is in language and thought closely parallel to what in the First Epistle to the Corinthians St. Paul affirms in general of the ministry in the Church, and of its analogue in the position of the several members in the human body (1 Cor. xii. 18, ὁ θεὸς ἔθετο τὰ μέλη ... ἐν τῷ σώματι : 28, οὓς μὲν ἔθετο ὁ θεὸς ἐν τῇ ἐκκλησίᾳ πρῶτον ἀποστόλους κ.τ.λ.; comp. 1 Thess. v. 9, 1 Tim. i. 12, ii. 7, 2 Tim. i. 11).

The idea of a divine appointment is in the apostolic writings expressed in different ways. What in the passage of the Corinthian Epistle just referred to is traced back to God the Father, is in a parallel passage of the Epistle to the "Ephesians" ascribed to the ascended Lord, the Mediator of the Father's activity in the Church (Eph. iv. 11). Here the appointment of the Elders is spoken of as the work of the Holy Ghost, that one Spirit who permeates and quickens the whole Body of Christ, and in whom there come to the Church the graces of fellowship and order (comp. 1 Cor. iii. 16, 2 Cor. xiii. 13, Phil. ii. 1, Eph. ii. 22, iv. 3). To the question, what precise form of the Spirit's action is in the speaker's mind, no certain answer can be given. The idea may be that the Church is the home and organ of the Holy Spirit, so that the action and thought of the Church or of its representatives may be rightly regarded as the action and thought of the Holy Spirit (xv. 28; comp. 1 Thess. iv. 8, 1 Cor. vii. 40). Or the allusion may be to utterances of Prophets speaking "in the Spirit," which had "led the way" to these members of the Church as fit to discharge the functions of rulers and teachers (1 Tim. i. 18, iv. 14, Acts xiii. 2). Or, lastly, the meaning may be that the manifestation in these men of the *charismata* of the Spirit (1 Cor. xii. 4 ff.) marked them out as able to bear the burden of the ministry. Any one of these thoughts, or a combination of them, may be the import of the phrase "in which the Holy Ghost set you as overseers"; and each of these thoughts is in harmony with those conceptions of the activities of the Holy Spirit which we find in St. Paul's Epistles.

The source of the ministry is above. What, then, is its special character? Those who are described in the narrative as "the elders of the church" (xx. 17; comp. Jas. v. 14) are here said to have been set in the flock as "overseers" (ἐπίσκοποι); their work was to "shepherd" the flock. Many points at once suggest themselves for discussion, but our treatment of these words must be limited by our immediate purpose, the comparison of the thoughts and language of this speech with the thoughts and language of the Pauline Epistles.

We take first the pastoral metaphor. The phrase "to feed (shepherd) my people Israel," or the like, is (in reference both to teaching and ruling) common in the Old Testament (*e.g.* 2 Sam. vii. 7, 1 Chron. xi. 2, Ps. lxxviii. 71, Jer. iii. 15); and the parable of the shepherd inspires notable passages of the Prophets (*e.g.* Jer. xxiii. 1 ff., Ezek. xxxiv.). The idea itself, and the group of words which express the idea, passed over into the Christian society, and were used with a recognized application to the life of the Church. The fact that St. Paul's metaphors are not commonly drawn from the fields (yet see 1 Cor. iii. 6 ff., ix. 7) emphasizes the occurrence of the word "shepherd" ($\pi o \iota \mu \acute{\eta} \nu$) in Eph. iv. 11 among terms denoting offices or aspects of the Christian ministry, and indicates that in such a connexion it had a definite and acknowledged meaning. In the passage of the speech at Miletus there is a very distinct transference of the language of the Old Testament to the Christian society. The flock which the shepherds are to tend is the redeemed congregation (τὴν ἐκκλησίαν τοῦ θεοῦ, ἣν περιεποιήσατο : Ps. lxxiv. 2, Is. xliii. 21), the new Israel (Gal. vi. 16, Rom. ii. 29, iv. 12, Phil. iii. 3, Titus ii. 14).

Closely connected with this pastoral language is the use here of the term "overseers" (ἐπίσκοποι). What is its relation to St. Paul's vocabulary? In his earliest Epistle (1 Thess. v. 12) the Apostle exhorts his converts to acknowledge "them that labour among you, and are over you (προϊσταμένους ὑμῶν) in the Lord, and admonish you." Here the allusion must be to the officers of the local Church, two departments of their "labour" being specially emphasized— that of ruling and that of teaching (comp. Eph. iv. 11, τοὺς δὲ ποιμένας καὶ διδασκάλους). This term (προϊστάμενοι), used in reference to the former of these functions, meets us again side by side with other specific terms—prophecy, ministry, teaching — in the Epistle to the Romans (xii. 8). Again, in the Pastoral Epistles the same word is definitely used in connexion with the work of the Elders (1 Tim. v. 17, *οἱ καλῶς προεστῶτες πρεσβύτεροι*). Here then we have a term which for St. Paul and for his converts had a recognized meaning; it expressed the activities of the Elders regarded as the rulers of a Church. A parallel term is that under discussion now—the term ἐπίσκοποι, the use of which in St. Paul's Epistles it is necessary for our present purpose, however briefly, to trace.

In the salutation of the Epistle to the Philippians (i. 1 f.) the Apostle greets "all the saints which are at Philippi, with the overseers and the deacons" (σὺν ἐπισκόποις καὶ διακόνοις). The omission of the article in such a formula as a salutation does not imply indefiniteness. Two distinct classes of persons at Philippi are named, "the overseers" and "the deacons," who are set over against the main body, the unofficial members, of the Philippian Church. Further, the mention of the "overseers" immediately precedes the mention of the "deacons"; and the "deacons" in the First Epistle to Timothy, written a very few years later, are certainly an order of ministers in the Church. The natural inference is that "overseers" is a term synonymous with "elders." This conclusion is confirmed when we turn to the Pastoral Epistles.

In the First Epistle to Timothy, after giving directions about the Christian assemblies and the place of men and women therein (ii. 1-15), the Apostle goes on to treat of the officers in the Church: "If a man seeketh overseership (ἐπισκοπῆς), he desireth a good work. The overseer (τὸν ἐπίσκοπον, *i.e.* each overseer) therefore must be without reproach, etc. . . . Deacons in like manner must be grave, etc."(iii. 1 ff.) Here again the reference to "deacons" precludes any indefiniteness in the interpretation of the terms "overseership" and "overseer." Moreover, the "overseer" must be "one that ruleth (προϊστάμενον) well his own house"; for, it is added, "if a man knoweth not how to *rule* (προστῆναι) his own house, how shall he *take care* (ἐπιμελήσεται) of the church of God?" Hence the office is obviously that of a ruler. Lastly, unless the term "overseer" is practically equivalent to the term "elder," we have the strange result that while directions are given as to the qualifications for the diaconate (iii. 8 ff.), and as to the treatment of Elders who are pre-eminent, and of those who fail, in their office (v. 17-19), nothing is said of the characteristics which are essentially needful in an Elder. It is very probable that the word ἐπισκοπή (which carries with it the τὸν ἐπίσκοπον of the following verse) is used in iii. 1, because there is no word corresponding to πρεσβύτερος which expresses the office. Again, in v. 17, "Let the elders that rule well (οἱ καλῶς προεστῶτες πρεσβύτεροι) be counted worthy of double honour," it is implied that government is the function of all Elders, but that those who excel in their office are to receive "double honour"; and, further, προεστῶτες takes up the idea of ἐπισκοπή, καλῶς προεστῶτες being virtually equivalent to καλῶς ἐπισκοποῦντες. The evidence of the corresponding passage in Titus (i. 5 ff.) is not less clear—"For this cause left I thee in Crete, that thou shouldest ... appoint elders in every city, ... if any man is blameless.... For the overseer [*i.e.* each man who holds the office of ruler just spoken of] must be blameless, as God's steward." The "for" appears absolutely to require that the class of church-officers referred to in the term "the overseer" should be that to which "the Elders" just mentioned belonged. It gives a reason for the direction implied in the words, "if any man is blameless," asserting (1) that that character is essentially necessary (δεῖ), and (2) that the reason of that necessity lies in the fact that the Elder is nothing less than "God's steward."

It seems, therefore, impossible to explain St. Paul's language in the Epistles to the Philippians and in the Pastoral Epistles, except on the supposition (1) that the term "overseer" (ἐπίσκοπος) denotes a primary and essential function of an "elder," and that therefore the two terms "elder" and "overseer" are synonymous; (2) that the word "overseer" had a definite meaning in St. Paul's vocabulary, and was recognized as such by those Christians in writing to whom he employs it. Whether or not it was at this early date a current term in other than Pauline Churches there is not sufficient evidence to shew.

When from this long digression we at length turn back to the passage in the Acts, we find that the use of the term "overseer" in the speech is entirely in harmony with St. Paul's use of it in the Epistles. Here it is doubtless part of the pastoral metaphor—a metaphor which had itself become part of the recognized language of the Church. The force of the word is greatly increased, if we suppose, as we have independent reasons for supposing, that at least in Pauline Churches it was a quasi-technical term, expressing the functions of government which were inseparable from the office of an "Elder." For it is when a term has a specific meaning that a skilful speaker or writer illuminates it by an allusion to its original meaning, and by weaving it into a context of metaphor (comp. 1 Cor. x. 2, Phil. iii. 2 f., Col. ii. 11, 1 Tim. v. 1, 1 Peter v. 1, 5).

The teaching of the speech as to the Church, in which the Elders were to labour, cannot be passed over in silence—"to feed the church of God which he purchased with the blood of his own [Son] (*v.* 28)." The phrase "the church of God," carrying upward the idea of the Christian society on earth, and immediately connecting that society with Him "from whom are all things," is common in St. Paul's writings,[1] and

---

[1] The expression is used by St. Paul (i.) of a local church, 1 Thess. ii. 14, 2 Thess. i. 4, 1 Cor. i. 2, xi. 16, 2 Cor. i. 1; (ii.) of the Universal Church, 1 Cor. x. 32, xv. 9, Gal. i. 13; (iii.) in passages where it is not clear whether the reference is local or universal, 1 Cor. xi. 22, 1 Tim. iii. 5, 15.

is found nowhere else in the New Testament. The descriptive words "which he purchased" appear to shew that the speaker has in mind the Universal Church spread throughout the world —"the blessed company of all faithful people." Hints of this conception of the Church appear in those Pauline Epistles which belong to the third missionary journey (1 Cor. x. 32, xii. 28, xv. 9, Gal. i. 13); it is the dominating thought of the Epistle to the "Ephesians." It must needs be that the Elders' service of the Universal Church was limited by their opportunities. They would truly minister to the whole flock if they ministered to that part of the flock which was committed to their care. The language in which the speaker refers to the Church as a possession acquired by God, closely allied to the apostolic language about redemption, and ultimately derived from the Old Testament (Ex. xv. 16, Ps. lxxiv. 2, Is. xliii. 21 (LXX.)), is not unfamiliar to the student of St. Paul's Epistles (Eph. i. 14, Titus ii. 14; 1 Cor. vi. 20, vii. 23, Rom. vi. 22). And here the generosity and beneficence of God's dealings with men are enhanced by the description of the price paid. That price is nothing less than "the blood of his own [Son]."

In the doctrine of the passage, when the text has been thus restored by what I venture to consider Dr. Hort's certain conjecture,[1] three points claim attention. (i.) These words complete the doctrine of the divine Sonship as expressed in the Pauline speeches (ix. 20, xiii. 33; see above, pp. 174 ff.). The Lord Jesus is the Son of God in a unique and absolute sense—the Father's "own Son." Such is the doctrine of St. Paul's Epistles (see p. 191, n.). (ii.) The passage is in complete conformity with St. Paul's habitual teaching about redemption. God the Father is the ultimate source of salvation. The work of salvation is His work. The Mediator through whom it is wrought out is the incarnate Son (*e.g.* 1 Thess. v. 9, 2 Cor. v. 18 ff., Rom. v. 8 ff., Col. i. 19 f., Eph. i. 5 ff., Titus ii. 11 ff.). In particular, stress is laid by St. Paul in the Epistles, as here, on the "blood" of Christ, His surrendered life, as the price of man's redemption from sin and of the divine purchase of man into a new

---

[1] Dr. Hort (*Introduction, Notes on Select Readings*, p. 99) suggests "that ΥΙΟΥ dropped out after ΤΟΥΙΔΙΟΥ at some very early transcription affecting all existing documents."

slavery (Rom. iii. 25, v. 9, Col. i. 20, Eph. i. 7, ii. 13). (iii.) Here we have an allusion to the Three Persons of the Trinity, not in Their eternal and essential relations, but as They are severally concerned in the regeneration of man. If the work of redemption is the work of the Father through the mediation of the Son, it is the Holy Spirit who dwells in and inspires the redeemed Church. For such devotional allusions to the Holy Trinity in St. Paul's Epistles, compare 2 Thess. ii. 13 f., 1 Cor. xii. 4 ff., 2 Cor. i. 21 f., xiii. 13, Gal. iv. 4 ff., Eph. iv. 4 ff.

Such is "the Church of God," for whose sake, in view of the dangers which were coming upon it, the Elders were to be wakeful and active. The charge laid upon them is "watch ye" (γρηγορεῖτε) — "verbum pastorale" (Bengel). The duty which in St. Paul's Epistles is enjoined on all Christian men (1 Thess. v 6, 1 Cor. xvi. 13, Col. iv. 2) is here spoken of as in a peculiar sense incumbent on the rulers of the Church (see 2 Tim. iv. 5 (νῆφε) compared with 1 Thess. v. 6, 8). If they ask for guidance in the fulfilment of this injunction, the Apostle points them to his example when he lived and worked at Ephesus.

This pastoral charge is immediately followed by the solemn words of final commendation: "And now I commend you to God, and to the word of his grace, even to him who is able to build up and to give the inheritance among all them that are sanctified[1]" (*v.* 32). The speaker entrusts (παρατίθεμαι) the Elders, with their future full of manifold dangers, and their present charged with responsibility and labour, to God. God will watch over them and guard them (comp. *e.g.* 1 Thess. iii. 12 f., 2 Thess. iii. 3, 1 Cor. i. 8, Rom. xvi. 25, Phil. iv. 19). In His hand they are placed as a precious deposit (παραθήκη, 2 Tim. i. 12). Nay, in a true and important sense, the Gospel which these teachers were to proclaim, the Gospel of God's universal benevolence in Christ, would for them, as they apprehended it themselves and announced it to others, become a saving power. God worked for their good through the very message which they were commissioned to deliver. But these words are, it seems probable, parenthetical. The dominating

---

[1] The words (τῷ δυναμένῳ ... πᾶσιν) appear to express a truth about God's dealing with His people generally.

thought is the protecting care of God, who was "able" (Rom. xvi. 25, Eph. iii. 20; 2 Cor. ix. 8, Rom. xiv. 4, 2 Tim. ii. 12) to "build up," and finally "to give the inheritance." The former of these two metaphors, that of building, is concerned with the present; it deals not so much with individuals as with the whole body of the faithful, its increase and its growing unity and cohesion (comp. 1 Cor. iii. 9 ff., Eph. ii. 20 ff., iv. 12 ff.). The second metaphor, that of the inheritance, refers to the future (Col. iii. 24, Eph. i. 14; comp. Heb. i. 14). The speaker looks forward to the final gathering together into the kingdom of God of " all them that are sanctified," all the heirs of the divine promises, whether under the old or under the new covenant (Eph. ii. 13 ff.). Christian men are already "fellow-citizens of the saints" (Eph. ii. 19); already, that is, they are joined in the heavenly polity with all those of old time who lived the life of faith. In God's good time "the number of the elect," of "all the saints" (1 Thess. iii. 13, 2 Thess. i. 10; comp. Eph. iii. 18), will be "accomplished." To that "day of Christ" God is "able" to bring His servants. These two closely related thoughts, faith in God's power to keep those that are His, and the assurance of "the reward of the inheritance" (Col. iii. 24), are, as here, brought together in a passage of St. Paul's Epistle to the "Ephesians" in which (as in our present passage) we catch an echo of Deut. xxxiii. 3 f.—"that ye may know what is the hope of your calling, what the riches of the glory of *his inheritance among the saints*, and what the exceeding greatness of *his power* ($\delta\upsilon\nu\acute{\alpha}\mu\epsilon\omega\varsigma$) to usward who believe (i. 18 f.)." The speaker's belief in the divine faithfulness towards those whom he commits to Him reaches onward to the time of the final consummation (1 Thess. ii. 19, iii. 13, 1 Cor. i 8, Phil. i. 6, 2 Tim. i. 12).

The missionary speeches which in the Acts are put into the mouth of St. Paul cover, as we have seen, a wide field. To the speech in the synagogue of Antioch and to the two speeches addressed to heathen, there is nothing analogous in the Epistles of St. Paul. The foregoing investigation of these speeches has, I trust, been thorough; I have not consciously avoided any topic which might seem to throw doubt on the position that they are ultimately the product of St. Paul's mind. But in the course of the discussion nothing has been discovered in regard either to language or to thought which, under the supposed circumstances, would have been unnatural in St. Paul as we know him in his letters. On the positive side, while these speeches are as far as possible removed from being mere centos of Pauline expressions, their phraseology and their ideas present frequent and delicate points of contact with the phraseology and ideas of St. Paul's Epistles. We here handle threads which we trace woven into the doctrinal and devotional fabric of the Apostle's writings. We discover in these speeches conceptions in a general and elementary form to which in the Epistles a matured expression is given, and which are there found in their theological context. A comparison of other New Testament documents justifies us in regarding these conceptions, in their earlier as in their later presentation, as characteristically Pauline.

A writer who was drawing on his own

imagination would almost inevitably have pictured the Apostle, on the few occasions when he recorded his supposed utterances, as proclaiming the essential truths of the Gospel, and as reaping a large harvest of converts. In the speech at Lystra, however, there is nothing —in the speech at Athens there is very little— which is distinctively Christian. At Lystra the only issue of the missionary's appeal is that the crowds were hardly dissuaded from offering sacrifice to him and his companion; at Athens, only "certain clave unto him, and believed." It is not too much to say that such speeches, with such meagre results, cannot be the invention of a romancer, of whose history St. Paul is the chief hero.

The speech at Miletus deals with a situation which has many points of similarity to the different occasions which called forth St. Paul's letters. We find, accordingly, as we should expect to find, that in this speech the language and the thoughts bear the closest resemblance to the language and the thoughts of St. Paul's Epistles. Moreover—and this is of still greater significance—in the speech and in the Epistles we discern the same religious temper and the same combination of human qualities—eagerness and tenderness, humility and self-assertion, steadfastness and awe in face of danger. In a word, the speech is inspired by that complex Pauline character which is familiar to the sympathetic student of the Epistles, but which defies exact analysis and definite statement.

It is, however, only when these speeches are regarded as a series that their evidential value is fully appreciated. We can imagine a disciple of St. Paul, or a student of St. Paul's writings, composing with fair success a controversial Pauline speech on the model of the Epistle to the Galatians, and a pastoral Pauline speech on the model of the Epistle to the Philippians. But to invent four Pauline speeches, for three of which the Epistles supply no pattern, each appropriate to its alleged occasion, each diverse from the other three, each congruous with St. Paul's character, each containing (though not all in the same proportion) resemblances, often subtle and always unobtrusive, to the style and phraseology of St. Paul's Epistles—this would have been a literary and psychological feat demanding extraordinary dramatic power. The "traditional" view of these Pauline speeches in the Acts is simple and adequate; it explains the phenomena. I venture to think that the unbiassed scholar, whether he regards the problem from the standpoint of the theologian or from that of the literary critic, will recognise St. Paul's mind, which we know in the Epistles, as the mind which finds expression in those speeches of the Acts which the writer of the Book puts into the mouth of that Apostle.

We have now completed the investigation to which in the first lecture I invited you. We have followed the writer of the Acts of the Apostles along the main road of history, which is traced out in the opening page of the Book. It remains that we should briefly review the ground which we have traversed.

The account of the events of the Day of Pentecost is felt by many to present serious difficulties. It would be too much to say that our examination of these problems has supplied a final solution in each case; but it has at least shewn that they are capable of a reasonable solution, and has moreover indicated the kind of solution to which further study and thought may be expected to attain.

The history of the growth of the Church, its expansion from Jerusalem to Rome, and the inclusion of Gentiles within its boundaries, is simple and natural, wholly unlike what would have been evolved out of the imagination of a romance-writer. The insignificance of the events which form the turning-points of the narrative, the existence in the record of obscurities, and the hints which it contains from time to time of an unrecorded background of history, are a strong guarantee of substantial truthfulness.

The speeches which are put into the mouth of the two great Apostles, St. Peter and St. Paul, are, in regard to doctrine, thought, and language, marked by wide differences. The teaching of St. Peter is in complete harmony with the alleged historical environment. It bears clear and emphatic testimony to the resurrection and exaltation of the Lord Jesus, and finds in these events a divine reversal of

Israel's act of condemnation and rejection. But it does not dwell on their spiritual significance. It moves within the circle of Jewish Messianic hopes and stands in striking contrast to the presentation of Christian truth found in the Apostolic Epistles. In a word, the Petrine speeches in the Acts exemplify a type of Christian thought which was tentative and immature, and which it would have been exceedingly difficult for a Pauline Christian, writing more than a quarter of a century later, to reproduce by an effort of the imagination.

The speeches of St. Paul, while they harmonize with the circumstances which are said to have called them forth, and while in substance and in tone they are widely separated from each other, all contain Pauline characteristics, and are such as might well have been the utterances of the Apostle whose letters we know. The silence of the two speeches addressed to heathen audiences as to details of Christian doctrine, though entirely explicable by the circumstances of their delivery, is a convincing argument against the theory that they are the invention of the writer. The Apostle's witness to Jews and to unconverted Gentiles could not have been manufactured on the model of St. Paul's Epistles, yet it is in harmony with the teaching of the Epistles, and touches on thoughts which are characteristic of St. Paul, and which in the Epistles are expounded in their theological context. The speech at Miletus, the matter of which is cognate with the matter of many passages of the Epistles, though it is not a mere echo of their phraseology, is in substance, in manner, and in spirit thoroughly and consistently Pauline.

Though, then, it is not denied that the speeches, more especially those of St. Peter, have been edited by the writer of the Acts and owe to him their present literary form, it has been shewn, I venture to think, that it is a moral impossibility for them to have been conceived and composed by him.

A reasonable account has been given of the preservation of the substance and (within certain limits) of the language of these discourses, if the author of the Acts be St. Luke. And further, if the "we-sections" of the Acts receive their natural interpretation, and the evidence of St. Paul's Epistles as to St. Luke be taken into account, it appears that the Evangelist was brought into personal communication with those who could give him full and trustworthy information as to each part of the history which he has included in his Book.

Thus the "traditional" view of the Book, which we know to have been that of the Christian society since the time of Irenæus, stands the test of careful and thorough investigation, and may claim to be accounted the "critical" view.

It is not of course maintained that the Book presents a full and faultless account of the period which it covers. The scientific critic, who on good grounds is assured of the general credibility of the Book, is ready and anxious to consider dispassionately the degree of accuracy which can be rightly ascribed to the record of any particular event.

The reference to Theudas in the speech of Gamaliel (v. 36 f.) is the most conspicuous example of one type among the problems of which no certain solution has yet been given. In that speech the rising of Theudas is explicitly spoken of as earlier in date than that of "Judas of Galilee in the days of the enrolment." But the date of "the enrolment" is A.D. 7; and the Theudas whom Josephus (*Antiq.* XX. v. 1) mentions was hunted down and beheaded in the procuratorship of Fadus (A.D. 44). The explanation of the difficulty given by Bishop Lightfoot and others—that Theudas is not an uncommon name, and that the Theudas of St. Luke is not the Theudas of Josephus, but "one of the many pretenders of whom Josephus speaks as troubling the peace of the nation about this time (Joseph. *Ant.* XVII. x. 8, *B.J.* II. iv. 1), without, however, giving their names"—is probably the true solution of the problem. But if, for the sake of argument, we disallow this and any similar explanation, and admit that in the speech of Gamaliel there is a serious chronological blunder, how does this admission affect the general credibility of the Acts? The history breaks off at Rome some two years after St. Paul's arrival there. From St. Paul's Epistles we know that St. Luke was with him in Rome during at least a portion of his captivity. These notices supply the only clue which we have as to the place and date of the composition of the Acts. If, then, we suppose that St. Luke wrote his Book after St. Paul's release and departure from the city, or after his death, it follows that the Book took its present shape when the author had lost the guidance of his chief authority. There is no reason to suppose that St. Luke had a minute acquaintance with the details of the tangled history of Judæa during the previous seventy years. And it might well be that, in filling out his notes of the account which he had received (probably from St. Paul) of Gamaliel's speech, he inserted the name of a Jewish insurgent which he happened to recall, but as to whose chronological position he was mistaken. At the worst, then, St. Luke appears guilty of ignorance as to the history of Judæa and of carelessness as an editor. We should not feel compelled to doubt the general trustworthiness of a historian of Indian missions if, writing at a distance and without access to documents and old newspapers, in an incidental allusion he made a serious blunder and confused two of the many native chieftains who from time to time have risen against English rule.

A much more serious question confronts us in the miraculous and supernatural element in the Book. Probably to many minds the real objection against the credibility of the Acts is to be found in such a history as that of the raising of Dorcas, or that of St. Peter's release from prison through the agency of an angel. It would be cowardly to bring this course of lectures to a close and leave this question or this group of questions unnoticed. My endeavour to deal with it must needs in some sense take the form of a confession of faith.

I believe that the life of our Lord Jesus Christ on earth stands absolutely apart from all other human lives; for I believe that, when He was conceived and born, the Word of God took flesh, and that for many years the Incarnate Word dwelt among men. This faith, received in early childhood, I hold to-day with conscious conviction, because toward it many lines of evidence — intellectual, moral, and spiritual—seem to me to converge. In particular, the Resurrection appears to me to be an historical event, resting on adequate testimony and confirmed by the life of the Church from the first day until now. I have not—I cannot have—any *a priori* notions of what the life on earth of God Incarnate would be. But since I believe that through the Word God is immanent in creation, it appears to me reasonable to expect that in the human life of the Incarnate Word there would be much transcending common experience. All the accounts of that Life affirm that He wrought miracles. My belief in the Divinity of the Lord Jesus Christ is not based on, is not even strengthened by, the miracles which are recorded of Him. I can believe the miracles, because I believe that He was God manifest in the flesh. That human life has a place absolutely unique. The miracles connected with that Life stand apart. I do not question that an intense faith in Him—allied to, but transcending, the power of the human will—may have been allowed at a crisis of revelation to produce effects which are denied to faith at other times. I am sure that the best men of that earliest Christian generation did believe that such effects were wrought (1 Cor. xii. 9 f., 28 ff., 2 Cor. xii. 12, Gal.

iii. 5, Rom. xv. 19, Hebr. ii. 4; comp. [Mark] xvi. 17 f., 20). But my spiritual and intellectual attitude towards the record of these miracles must be different from my spiritual and intellectual attitude towards the record of the miracles of our Lord Jesus Christ. It would be no shock to my faith as a Christian, if I felt assured that the author of the Book of the Acts or his informants, having the events of the Lord's life on earth vividly before their minds, gave a supernatural interpretation to what were in truth providential interventions within what we term the sphere of the natural order. Beyond this point I find it impossible to go in the direction either of affirmation or of denial.

If, then, the Book of the Acts suggests problems, historical, psychological, and religious, towards which we must be content to stand in the attitude of suspended judgment, we may, I believe, approach the further consideration of these questions, and wait for further evidence and for fuller light, assured that there speaks to us in that Book an honest and well-informed Christian man, the companion and friend of St. Paul—St. Luke, "the beloved physician."

Little did I think, when hardly more than two months ago I invited you to consider the subject which we have just laid aside, that this course of lectures would conclude on a Sunday so memorable, so sadly memorable, as this.

We know, but we scarcely realize, that since last Sunday the longest, the greatest, probably the most eventful reign in all English history has ended. We know, but we scarcely realize, that the Queen whom our parents, when they were still young, learned to reverence and love, and whom they taught us to reverence and love, loyalty towards whom has deepened with the knowledge and the convictions of maturer years, has passed away. We often wondered what it would be when the Queen was taken from her people. But we always put the thought quickly away. We had never known our country apart from our Queen. It did not seem possible that we should ever so know it. At last the inevitable hour has come.

Once or twice in a lifetime there is given to most of us that strange experience, that sad but almost triumphant thankfulness, that wonderful mingling of sorrow and of peace, with which we look back over a long and useful life brought at length to its full completeness. It is so now. We mourn the Queen to-day with the mourning of sons and daughters.

We cannot say much. We are oppressed with a sense of the indignity of hasty words, of the poverty and inadequacy even of rightful words. History, when the secrets of the great crises of the Queen's reign and of the part she bore in them are fully disclosed to our children and our children's children—history will pass its calm and impartial verdict on the Queen. We cannot read that verdict now. We do not fear what that verdict will be.

Yet, even here and now, we cannot but give expression to some simple and obvious thoughts.

We think of the greatness, the true greatness, of the Queen's life. The voice of vulgar adulation is hushed in the presence of Death. But what I venture to say is within the limits of the soberest truth. The life through the providence of God has been great in its opportunity. The current of national and imperial change which has flowed so strong during the last seventy years, might have been broken into dangerous eddies had it struck upon the rock of a headstrong sovereign's prejudices. It has been guided and controlled and calmed by the unobtrusive influence of a woman's tact, trained, as decade after decade has passed by, by a ripening experience and knowledge of affairs, unique in the annals of monarchy. The life has been great in the qualities which all now recognize — a strong will curbed by a deep and religious sense of overwhelming obligations; an instinctive perception of the *feeling* of her people; a keen enjoyment of all that was good and wholesome in English life, yet which never used the prerogatives of power as a means for securing personal gratification; a royal mind which recognised the awful seriousness of sovereignty, but which was never so overwhelmed with imperial cares as to forget to rejoice with those of her subjects who rejoiced, and to weep with those of them who wept; and these qualities rooted and fixed in the fear and in the love of God.

We think of the compass of the Queen's life. The reign began almost on the morrow of the Reform Bill. It has been prolonged into a new century. And all the changes in Church and State during those many years —changes the issues of which have been the confirmed stability of our great institutions—the Queen watched, always, we are told, labouring for peace, always controlling her personal judgment by a scrupulous observance of the limits of a constitutional monarchy. And if we take a wider view, we remember how the Queen presided over the reorganization and development of England's vast Indian Empire; how she fostered the growth of English colonies, till from little more than straggling and rude settlements they have become mighty commonwealths, bound to each other and bound to the Mother Country by ties of a common loyalty, ties knit more firmly by the common sacrifices of the last year and by the common grief of to-day. Nor can we forget the smaller world of the University, so dear to ourselves.

The era of the Queen's reign has been an era of change to Cambridge. Twice in her reign —once, indeed, when her royal Consort was our Chancellor — did her Majesty give her sanction to statutes which essentially modified the constitution of the University as it had been ordained nearly three centuries earlier by the Statutes of Elizabeth. But legislative enactments, I need not remind you, are no measure of the transformation, the happy transformation, which has passed over the aims, the methods, and the social life of this place since the Queen's accession. We have but to review the history of our own University, and we learn something of the compass of the Queen's life.

We think of the completeness of the Queen's life. It has been complete in all the sacred relations of an English home—the life of the wife, the mother, the ancestress of royal houses; complete and perfected by many sorrows—even, we dare to say, by that signal sorrow which for forty years has left "the Crown a lonely splendour"; complete in the scarcely less sacred relations of the larger household of the nation, *known* to be complete when the two great jubilee thanksgivings revealed to all the world the Queen's trust and pride in her people, and the people's trust and pride in their Queen. The life we may now reverently pronounce as happy, happy in its completeness.

And now in the midst of these solemn days when the past and the future of English history — the past with its wonderful blessings, the future with its unknown possibilities — conspicuously meet before our eyes, we bring our grief and our hope into the presence of Almighty God.

We pray—for we are sure that the Queen often so prayed, and would have wished us so to pray—for the Empire, that God will make this great national sorrow a wholesome discipline to chasten and to correct our sins and shortcomings in Church and in State,—our pride, our waywardness, our luxury, our forgetfulness of God; that, as sometimes, when the sun has set, we are still conscious of his influence in the soft twilight of holy calm, so in her own England and in the world the remembrance of the Queen may be a power making for peace, so that to her very memory may be vouchsafed the blessing of the peace-makers.

We pray—for we are sure that the Queen often so prayed, and would have wished us so to pray—for him who has now become our King, that he may reign over us, as she reigned so long, in the faith and fear of God, supported by God's strength and guidance, upheld by wise and patriotic counsellors, loved and honoured by his subjects.

And for her—for her long reign, for her goodness, for her wisdom, for the purity of her Court and the white stainlessness of her life, for her example, for her unstinted service of her own generation—yes, and even for this, that by the will of God she fell asleep without the sorrow of a long decay, we thank God.

INDEX

Acts of the Apostles, date, 9, 28, 297 f.; place of composition, 297 f.; relation to St. Luke's Gospel, 6 f., 16 f.; plan, 29 f.; gaps in the writer's knowledge, 24 f., 27; relation to the Epistles of St. Paul, 26 f., 91 ff., 168-292 *passim*, 294 f.; passages commented on, i. 1, p. 52; i. 3 ff., p. 29; i. 8, pp. 47 ff.; ii. 17, p. 59; ii. 22, p. 142; ii. 23, p. 147; ii. 33 f., p. 151; ii. 36, pp. 123 f., 154 ff.; ii. 39, p. 59; iii. 13, p. 124; iii. 14, pp. 132 ff.; iii. 16, p. 121; iii. 25, p. 124; iii. 26, p. 60; vii. 52, pp. 133 ff.; viii. 1, pp. 49 f.; viii. 39, p. 67 n.; ix. 20 ff., pp. 174, 177; ix. 31, p. 50; ix. 32, p. 75; x. 11 ff., pp. 78 f.; xi. 18, p. 80; xi. 19, pp. 82 ff.; xi. 28, p. 5; xiii. 2, p. 86; xiii. 17, p. 179; xiii. 29, p. 184 n.; xiii. 32 ff., pp. 187 ff.; xiii. 34 f., pp. 180 ff.; xiii. 39, pp. 191 ff.; xiii. 46 ff., p. 89; xv. 23 ff., pp. 93 ff.; xvii. 18, pp. 204 f.; xvii. 19, pp. 207, 209; xvii. 22, pp. 212 f.; xvii. 23, pp. 216 f.; xvii. 26, pp. 222 f.; xvii. 28, pp. 225 f.; xvii. 30, p. 221 n.; xx. 18, p. 236; xx. 20, 27, pp. 254 ff.; xx. 28, pp. 271, 273 ff.; xx. 29, pp. 263 f.; xx. 30, pp. 268 ff.; xx. 32, pp. 286 ff.; xxii. 14, pp. 133 ff.; xxiv. 2 ff., p. 111; xxviii. 28, p. 100; xxviii. 31, pp. 100 f.

Agora, the, at Athens, 204 f., 209
Altar (ἀγνώστῳ θεῷ), 216 f.
Antioch in Pisidia, 89; St. Paul's speech at, 179 ff.
Antioch, the Syrian, 5, 81, 84, 90
Apocalypse, xxii. 20, p. 155 n.
Apostles, dispersion of the, 75
Aramaic, 154
Aratus, 226 n.
Archæology, 7 f.
Areopagus, the, 207 ff.
Athens, St. Paul's speech at, 204 ff., 290; St. Paul's silence as to Christian doctrine at, 231 f.; small success at, 233 f.
ἀκωλύτως, 101
ἀνάστασις, misunderstood by the Athenians, 205 f.
ἀναστῆσαι, 188 n.
ἄνδρες ἀδελφοί, 123
ἀρχηγός, 129 f.
ἄφιξις, 263 ff.

Background of facts implied, 33, 75, 151 f., 180
Baptism, the, of the Lord, 141, 189
Baruch, Apocalypse of, 55, 65, 124, 136, 192, 199
Benedictions, the Eighteen, 39, 124. 130 ff., 139
Bengel, 232, 269 f., 285

Bezae, Codex, 5
Blasphemy, the Lord crucified for, 148 f.
Blass, Prof., 5 f., 205 n.
Blood, 95 f.; the Blood of Christ, 284 f.
"Brethren," 94 f.
Building, metaphor of, 287
Burial, the, of the Lord, 184

Cæsarea, 79
"Cevennes, The Little Prophets of the," 38 n.
Charles, Dr., 176 n.
Christ, the Person of, 125 ff., 135, 140, 154 ff., 174 ff., 187 ff., 232, 282 ff., 299 f.
"Christian," the name, 84 ff.
Chronology, the, of the Acts, 68 n.
Chrysostom, 207 n.
Church, the, the new Israel, 48 f., 277; as God's own possession, 283; "the Church (Churches) of God," 282
Circumcision, controversy about, 90 ff.
Cleanthes, 226
Clement of Alexandria, 10, 101
Clement of Rome, 140
Collection, the, for the poor at Jerusalem, 257 ff.
Colossæ, false teaching at, 269
Colossians, Epistle to the, ii. 1, p. 236
Comparative, the, quasi-superlative force of, 213 n.
Contemporary Review, 38 n.
Conversion of Saul of Tarsus, 69 ff.
Cook, Mr. A. B., 206 n.
Corinthians, the, questions of, 97; gift of tongues among, 36 ff.; First Epistle to, i. ii., pp. 233 f.; i. 1 f., p. 95; vii. 10, p. 252; xii. 3, p. 149; xv. 8, p. 72; xv. 32, p. 238; xv. 54 f., p. 181; xvi. 9, p. 238; Second Epistle to, general tone, 246 ff.; ii. 17, iv. 2, pp. 253 f.

Cornelius, 79 f.
Creed, the earliest Christian, 157
Creighton, Bishop, 159 ff.
Curtius, Dr. E., 207 n.
Cyprus, 86 f.

Dalman, Prof., 39 n., 127 f., 132 n., 134, 136, 139 n., 154 n., 156
Damascus, St. Paul's preaching at, 174 ff.
Deuteronomy, xii. 15, p. 79; xxi. 22 f., pp. 148 ff., 183 ff.
Diary of travel, 11
Didaché, the, 140, 155
Diognetus, Epistle to, 140
Dispersion, the, 60, 94, 123
Divinity, the, of Jesus Christ, 158, 174 ff., 190 f., 284 f. 299 f.
Documents, possible use of, in Acts, 8, 15 f., 120
Driver, Dr., 136 n.
δεισιδαίμων, 212 n.
διασπαρῆναι, 65

Edersheim, Dr., 31, 134, 136, 199 n.
Elymas, 86 f.
Enoch, Book of, 55, 133 f., 146, 175 f., 265
"Ephesians," Epistle to the, 23
Ephesus, St. Paul's long stay at, 236; his trials at, 237 ff.
Epistles, the, of St. Paul, relation to Acts, 26 f., 91 ff., 168-292 *passim*
Esdras, Second Book of, 145 f., 176, 192 f., 265
Eunuch, the Ethiopian, 66 f.
Evidence, the, of the Resurrection and Exaltation, 152 f., 185 f.
Ewald, 123
Exaltation, the, of the Lord, 150 ff.
Ezekiel, ii. 1, p. 71; iv. 14, p. 79
ἐγείρειν, 188 n.
ἐκδημῆσαι, ἐνδημῆσαι, 264
ἐπίσκοποι, 275 ff.
ἐπὶ τὸ αὐτό, 31
ἕως ἐσχάτου τῆς γῆς, 50 f.

INDEX

Fadus, the Procurator, 297
False teachers, 268 ff.
Field, Dr. F., 213 n.
Frazer, Dr. J. G., 206 n., 209 n., 216 n.

Galatia, Province of, 89
Galatians, Epistle to the, i. ii., pp. 91 ff.; i. 15 f., pp. 72 f., 177; ii. 9, p. 74; iii. 10, 13, p. 181
Galen, 112 n.
Gentiles, the, Jewish view of, 54 ff., 80, 88, 90 ff.; the Lord's relation to, 56 f.; call of, 67 ff., 79 f.; position in the Church, 90 ff.
Glossolalia, 35 ff.
Gospel according to St. Luke, the, Preface of, 16 ff.; relation to the Acts, 6 f., 16 ff.
Grace, the Jewish, 39, 199
Greek spoken in Palestine, 114 ff.

Habakkuk, i. 5, ii. 4, pp. 194 f.
Habinenu, 139
Hanging, death by, on a tree, 148 ff., 183 ff.
Harnack, Prof., 9 n., 28
Hastings, Dr., *Dictionary of the Bible*, articles on Acts, 8 n.; on Joppa, 77 n.; on *Maranatha*, 155 n.; on St. Mark, 22 n., 87; on St. Peter, 22 n., 75 n., 115 n., 176 n.; on 1 Peter, 115 n.
Hawkins, Sir J., 12 f.
Headlam, Mr. A. C., 8 n., 222
Heathen world, the, 202 f., 210 ff.; God's dealings with, 217 ff.
Hebrews, Epistle to the, use of LXX. in, 116; xiii. 22, p. 179 n.
Hellenists and Hebrews, 62, 119, 137 ff.
Hippolytus, 10
History, philosophy of, 225
Hobart, Dr., 13 f.
Holy, the, One, 132 ff.
Hort, Dr., 95, 98 f., 269, 284

James, St., 21, 76, 93; Epistle of, use of LXX. in, 116
James, Dr. M. R., 131 n.
Iaso, the goddess, 205 n.
Idolatry, 95 ff., 202 f.; St. Paul's view of, 210 ff.
Jebb, Sir R. C., 213 n.
Jeremiah, a type of St. Paul, 71
Jerusalem, 49, 51 f.; "Council" at, 90 ff.; St. Paul's journey to, 257 ff.
Jews, the, plots of, 238 ff.
Ignorance of the heathen, 214 ff.
Immanence, the divine, in the world, 227 f.
Inheritance, metaphor of, 287
John, St., Gospel according to, xx. 19 ff., p. 41; First Epistle of, ii. 1, 20, p. 135
Joppa, 77
Josephus, 30, 79, 84, 144, 148, 264 n., 297
Jowett, Prof., 198 n.
Irenæus, 10, 23, 296
Isaiah, vi. 9 f., pp. 99 f.; xlii. 1 ff., p. 138; xliii. 9 ff., p. 47; xlix. 6, p. 50; lv. 3, p. 182
Isis, 205 n.
Israel, Jehovah's son, 175; "the whole house of Israel," 123 f.; "*this* people Israel," 179 f.
Judas of Galilee, 296 f.
Judges, Book of, 129 f.
Judgment, the final, 231, 287
Jülicher, Prof., 9, 107
Justification, doctrine of, 191 ff.
Justin Martyr, 189
'Ιησοῦς, connected by the Athenians with ἴασις (ἴησις), 205 n.
'Ιουδαία, 49 n.

Kaddish, the, 124
King, the, of Israel, Jehovah's son, 175, 188 f.
Kirkpatrick, Dr., 136 n.
Κύριος, 154 ff.

Lamentations, Book of, iv. 20, p. 156

Language, the, of St. Peter's speeches, 114 ff.
Lessons read in the synagogue, 180
Letter, the, of the "Council" at Jerusalem, 93 ff.
Lightfoot, Bishop, 212, 230, 268 n., 297
Lord (our Lord), 154 ff.
Lord's sayings, the, early collection of, 251 ff.
Lots, use of, 42
Luke, St., in St. Paul's Epistles, 11; at Jerusalem and in Palestine, 20 f.; at Rome, 21, 297; a Gentile, 92; possibly able to use shorthand, 112 n.; acquainted with medical phraseology, 13 f.; changes the form of the Lord's sayings in the Gospel, 109 f.
Luther, 26
Lystra, St. Paul's speech at, 195 ff., 290; St. Paul silent as to Christianity, 203 f.

Maccabees, the, First Book of, xiv. 5, p. 77; Second Book of, i. 1, pp. 94 f.; Third Book of, vii. 18, p. 264 n.; Fourth Book of, 123
Mar, 154 ff.; *Marana*, 155; *Maranatha*, 155 n.
Mark, St., "interpreter" of St. Peter, 116; probably an informant of St. Luke, 21 f., 77, 87 f.
Matthew, St., Gospel according to, xii. 18 ff., p. 138
Matthias, St., choice of, 42
Medical language, use of, in the Acts, 13 f.
Messiah, the, Jewish hope of, 125 ff.; relation to the Messianic people, 126, 134, 176; predestination of, 146; "Son of God," 174 ff.; suffering and death of, 145, 178, 234
Miletus, St. Paul's speech at, 235 ff., 290 f.; how preserved, 112, 170 f.
Milman, Dean, 162 f.

Ministry, the Lord's, 141; the Christian, 271 ff.
Miracles, the Lord's, 142 f., 299 f.; in Judæa, 143 f.; significance of, 143 f.; in the Apostolic age, 299 ff.
Muratorian fragment on the Canon of N.T., 10

Nations, the, relation of, to Israel, 54 ff.; see also *Gentiles*
Nature, different views of, 200 f.; witness of, to God, 198 ff.

ὀθόνη, 78
οἶκος, 31 f.
ὡς, 213 n.

Pastoral Epistles, the, imply St. Paul's release, 262 f.; the false teaching combated in, 269; Christian ministry described in, 277 ff.
Pastoral office, the, self-discipline needed, 271 f.; catholic, 272; source, 273 ff.; character, 275 ff.
Paul, St., persecutor, 65, 266 f.; conversion of, 68 ff.; different elements in the work of 168 f.; as evangelist, 168; as an Apostle to Israel, 74; as Apostle of the Gentiles, 71, 73, 88; at Damascus, 174 ff.; at Antioch in Syria, 81 ff., 90; in Cyprus, 86 f.; becomes chief of the missionary band, 87; at Perga, 88 ff.; at Antioch in Pisidia, 89, 179 ff.; at Lystra, 195 ff.; controversy as to circumcision, 90 ff.; at Thessalonica, 197, 230, 246 ff.; at Athens, 204 ff.; at Corinth, 233 f.; at Ephesus, 236 ff.; collection for the Saints at Jerusalem, 98 f., 260 ff.; at Miletus, 234 ff.; at Rome, 23, 52, 99 f.; release from his Roman captivity, 262 f.; at Ephesus, 262; probably ignorant of parts

INDEX

of Gospel history, 184 f. ; knowledge of our Lord's sayings, 251 f. ; no sense of beauty of nature, 198 ; love for Israel, 239 ; diligence in manual work, 249 f. ; teacher of spiritual "wisdom," 255 f. ; of common duties, 256 f. ; language about death, 263 f. ; love for "all the flock," 272 ; method of quotation from O.T., 180 ff. ; sense of importance of history, 19'; St. Luke's informant, 19 f., 69, 120, 171 f. ; "theology" of, 174 ff., 189 ff., 227 f., 282 ff.

Paul, St., speeches of, selection in Acts, 171 f. ; as a series, 291 f. ; how preserved, 111 ff. ; compared with St. Peter's speeches, 169, 177, 184 ff., 187, 293 f. ; with St. Paul's Epistles, *e.g.* 194, 200 ff., 210 ff., 220 f., 227 ff., 238 ff., 243 ff., 257 ff., 271 ff., 289 ff., 294 f.

Pentecost, the Day of, 30 ff., 114, 117, 292 f. ; significance of, 40 ff.

Perga, 87 ff.

Persecution, 65, 265 ff.

Peter, St., at Jerusalem, 59 ff., 122 ff. ; leaves Jerusalem, 75 ff. ; at Joppa, 77 ff. ; at Cæsarea, 79 ff. ; at Rome, 22 ff., 121

Peter, St., speeches of, as a series, 122 ; original language, 114 ff. ; how preserved, 117 ff. ; St. Peter possibly St. Luke's informant, 22 ff., 121 ; relation to 1 Peter, 121 ; relation to Pauline speeches, 169, 185, 187, 293 f. ; their doctrinal character, 158 f., 293 f.

Peter, St., First Epistle of, i. 21, p. 121

Pharisees, the, 63

Philip the Evangelist, 20, 66 ff.

Philippians, Epistle to the, i. 1, p. 278

Plato, 228

Plumptre, Dean, 38 n.

Polycarp, martyrdom of, 140

Prayers, Jewish, 124, 134, 137 n., 139, 155 n.

Predestination of the Messiah, 146 f.

Preface to St. Luke's Gospel, 16 ff.

Promise, the Messianic, 188

Psalms, ii. 7, pp. 188 f. ; xvi. p. 185 ; lxvii. (lxviii.) 19, p. 151

Psalms, the, of Solomon, 51, 55, 124, 130 f., 133, 142, 146, 156, 187 n.

$παῖς$, 137 ff.

$παρακλήσεως$, $λόγος$, 179 n.

$πλῆθος$, 32

$ποιμήν$, 276 ff.

$προϊστάμενοι$, $οἱ$, 277 f.

Quotation from O.T., St. Paul's method of, 180 ff.

Rabbonana, 155

"Raise up, to," 129, 188 n.

Ramsay, Prof., 7, 36, 208 n.

Readings, discussion of, 5, 81 ff., 187 n., 284

Redemption, 282 ff.

Resch, Dr., 189 n.

Righteous One, the, 132 ff.

Romans, the Epistle to the, i. 1, 7, p. 95 ; i. 3 f., p. 190 ; iii. 25 f., pp. 219 ff. ; vii. viii., pp. 191 f. ; xv. 30 ff., pp. 258 f.

Rome, 21 ff., 51 f., 85, 99 ff., 297 f.

Ryle, Bishop H. E., 131 n.

Salmon, Dr., 6

Samaria, 49, 66

Samuel, Second Book of, vii. 12, p. 188

Sanday, Dr., 222 n.

Saviour (salvation), 129 ff., 284 f.

Schoettgen, 77 n.

Schürer, Dr., 39 n., 180

Septuagint, the, 13, 116, 138, 181 f.

Servant, the, of the Lord, 135 ff.

Shema, the, 39, 122 f.

Shepherd, the metaphor of the, 276 f.

Shorthand, use of, 111 f.
Sibylline Oracles, 130
Smith, Prof. G. A., 77 n.
Smith, Prof. Robertson, 96
"Son of God," 174 ff., 187 ff., 284
Sources of the Acts, 8, 14 ff., 110 ff., 171 f., 195 f., 295 f.
Spirit, the Holy, 40 ff., 141 f., 153, 273 ff.
Stephen, St., 62 f.; speech of, 182 f.
Stoics, the, 205, 214, 223, 226 f., 229
Strangled, things, 95 f.
Swete, Dr., 34 n., 116 n.
σπερμολόγος, 205 n.
σωτήρ (σωτηρία), 206 n.

Tanner, trade of a, 77
Targum, 136
Taylor, Dr. C., 155 n.
Temple, the, the place of the Pentecostal gift, 30 ff.
Tertullian, 10, 86
Text, the, of the Acts, 5 ff., 81 ff., 187 n., 284
Thayer, Dr., 155 n.
Theclae, Acta, 140, 204
Thessalonica, St. Paul's preaching at, 230
Theudas, 296 ff.
"*This* people Israel," 179 f.
Timothy, First Epistle to, iii. 1 ff., p. 279; v. 17, p. 280; vi. 3, p. 252

Titus, Epistle to, i. 5 ff., pp. 280 f.
Tongues, "like as of fire," 33 ff.; the gift of, 35 ff.
Trinity, work of the Holy, in man's salvation, 285
Tübingen School, 8 f.
τίθεσθαι, 273 f.

Unity, of the human race, 40, 222 ff.; of the Church, 91

Victoria, Queen, death of, 167, 302 ff.
Visions, St. Peter's vision, 78; in connexion with St. Paul's conversion, 70 n.
Voice at the Baptism and Transfiguration, 138

"Watch," 285
"We-sections," 5, 11 ff., 295 f.
Westcott, Bishop, 39 n., 70 n., 200 n.
Westcott and Hort, 187 n., 189 n.
"Western" text, the, 5 f.
Wetstein, 77 n.
Wisdom, Book of, used by St. Paul, 221 n.; ii. 12-20, pp. 137 f.
Witnesses, the Apostles as, 47
Wolves, metaphor of, 265
Wright, Rev. A., 38 n.

Zahn, Prof., 6, 26
Zeller, 226
Zöckler, Dr., 8 n.

THE END

www.ingramcontent.com/pod-product-compliance
Lightning Source LLC
Chambersburg PA
CBHW071231230426
43668CB00011B/1383